INTERNATIONAL TRADE AND ECONOMIC GROWTH

INTERNATIONAL TRADE AND ECONOMIC GROWTH

By

Dr. M. Lakshmi Narasaiah
M.A., Ph.D.

Professor of Economics
Co-ordinator, Dept. of M.B.A. and Commerce
Special Officer
Sri Krishnadevaraya University Post-graduate Centre
Kurnool–518 002
Andhra Pradesh
(India)

DISCOVERY PUBLISHING HOUSE PVT. LTD.
NEW DELHI-110 002

First Published - 2008

Reprinted - 2016

ISBN: 978-81-8356-305-5

International Trade and Economic Growth

Published by:

DISCOVERY PUBLISHING HOUSE PVT. LTD.
4383/4B, Ansari Road, Darya Ganj
New Delhi-110 002 (India)
Phone: +91-11-23279245, 43596064-65
Fax: +91-11-23253475
E-mail: discoverypublishinghouse@gmail.com
sales@discoverypublishinggroup.com
web: www.discoverypublishinggroup.com

Printed at:
Infinity Imaging Systems
Delhi

Preface

When trade policies are discussed nationally or internationally people as consumers are largely forgotten. Despite their numbers, they do not carry the weight that producers and other lobbies command. Individually, consumers are seldom informed about how the availability, quality, price and choice of the hundreds of items which they buy in the shops each year are affected by trade policy decisions. If they know-how much of their household budgets are determined by decisions to protect individual industries and for how little effect they might be shocked.

Equally, when it is debated publicly, the benefits that would fall to the consumers are usually ignored. This brief study is an attempt to put the consumer interest squarely in the public arena.

How Do Government Decisions on Trade Affect the Consumer?

Virtually all protective policies mean higher prices for the consumer. And if it is not a consumer who pays, it will be domestic producer. These are some of the main actions taken by national authorities.

Governments frequently and for the most part, legally raise revenue and protect domestic industries by imposing duties on imported products. If a product has a 25 per cent tariff, the price in the shop will normally be 25 per cent more than its price at the port or airport.

Global quotas and other numerical limits on imports are sometimes legal sometimes not. Either way the intention is to restrict access to the market in such a away that domestic producers of the same product can raise their prices without being forced out of business through lack of competitiveness. Quotas are frequently preferred by those demanding protection because the impact on prices is less obvious than with a tariff. Once again, prices go up in the shops and limits may be so narrow that goods disappear from the shelves altogether.

Voluntary export restraints are quotas of an even more costly kind for the importing country. They allow foreign suppliers to charge higher prices than would be possible under a tariff or normal quota. By "bribing" the exporter this way, opposition to the protection is reduced.

Subsidies are sometimes paid to domestic producers to help them compete with import competition by keeping their costs artificially low. This keeps prices down. Unfortunately, the consumer as a tax payer ends up paying for the subsidy. In so doing, he is prevented from keeping more of his income to spend on other goods, which may be produced by more efficient industries. One thing is sure once industries get used to subsidies, it is very hard to wean then away.

Rules permit governments to impose extra duties on imports where products are shown to be dumped (sold below the normal price in the exporting country) or subsidised, and where the effect of dumping or subsidisation is demonstrated to damage the corresponding domestic industry. While these duties may be justified, they nevertheless always serve to raise the price for consumers to knock products completely out of the market. Yet very few, if any, countries give much weight to consumer interest when deciding whether to impose such penalty duties. And their use had grown disturbingly in recent years.

Governments usually impose standards of safety, quality, public health and environmental protection for good reasons often in the interests of consumers. Sometimes, however, the standards and the procedures which enforce them are no more than hidden protection for domestic producers. In imposing unnecessary measures on imports, governments penalize consumers through higher prices and the non-availability of goods.

Dr. M. Lakshmi Narasaiah

Contents

1

World Trade—The Next Challenge

On 15 December 1993 the world changed. My be not as dramatically as the moment when the Berlin Wall fell, but then unlike that very necessary demolition job, the success of the Uruguay Round was a work of construction. Like the destruction of the wall, though, its effects will be profound and lasting ones felt far beyond its immediate context. It will be seen as a defining moment in modern history.

The importance of the Round can be seen in terms of boost it gives to job creation; to development; to investment; to economic reform; to the rule of law and in many other ways besides. All of these benefits are real and important. But the true value of the whole is much, much more than the sum of these parts.

Put simply, governments came to the conclusion that the notion of a new world order was not merely attractive but absolutely vital; that the reality of the global market—whatever ambitions some of them may retain for regional integration—required a level of multilateral cooperation never before attempted.

No Losers in the Round

It has created a revolutionary framework for economic, legal and political cooperation. But now turn to the immediate results of the Round. Seeing them as a profit and loss account or a scorecard of winners and losers is to see them in static terms, as one-off conclusions with finite effects. This misses the point completely.

Every nation now needs an effective trading system, but especially so the small and poor. They have it. Everyone will also gain from the huge package of market access results even if they did not get every concession they were seeking from trading partners—it is the biggest market access deal ever negotiated.

However, the essence of the Uruguay Round's achievements is that they are dynamic. The new agreements, the new rules and structures it sets up—all mean a commitment to a continuing process of cooperation and reform of which the agreement in December was only the beginning.

Maintaining the liberalising momentum will call for continuing effort and vigilance by participating countries. But now their energy can be focused through the Round's greatest innovation; the new World Trade Organisation (WTO) in place of the improvised basis on which the GATT has operated for 45 years, trade will now have a permanent forum appropriate to its importance in the world economy.

Technically speaking, the WTO will oversee the implementation of the Round's results, administer all the agreements in goods, services and intellectual property, and manage the unified dispute settlement system. But beyond these administrative functions, it will raise the political profile of trade a profile which has already been lifted greatly by the Uruguay Round. The WTO will have regular instead of occasional—direct Ministerial involvement. It will have a clear mandate to act as a forum for further trade negotiations. Most of all it will complete the transition from a trading system which largely restricted itself to policies at the border to one which also covers most aspects of domestic policy-making affecting international competition in goods and services, as well as investment.

Through the WTO, the Round will change the way the world economy is shaped. But it is not the final victory over protectionism and unilateralism. Any premature rejoicing would have quickly been cut short by the evidence since 15

December that major economic powers are still ready to take the unilateral approach to trade problems. Arguments for protectionism based on the alleged threat of low-cost competition to production and jobs will not just fade away because the Round is a success. The seductive appeal of "beggar-thy-neighbour" policies is highlighted by the seemingly greater vigour of the lobbies for protectionism than the advocates of open markets.

These dangers—and the speed with which they have resurfaced—make the achievement of the Uruguay Round all the more important, and its successful implementation all the more urgent. Implementation requires more than mutual backslapping about what we have achieved. It requires now that the US, EU and Japan, in particular, rapidly obtain final authority to ratify and also take a lead in providing the WTO with the means to fulfil its mandate.

The success of the Round has come at a time when it is even more vitally needed than anyone could have guessed when it was launched in 1986. Old structures and alignments have been turned inside out in trade as in every other area of international relations. We face a world of change and challenge, in which the reinforced trading system will be a primary source of stability and security.

The developing countries including India have become enthusiastic supporters of the multilateral trading system and the Uruguay Round even if all their demands were not met by industrial countries. The reasons lie in the changing economic policies of many developing countries and the clearer appreciation of the value of the GATT system that has grown along with these changes.

The challenge of new issues in World Trade will be a major one for the WTO. The new organisation has to consider issues such as the links between trade and the environment, international competition policy, trade and investment, and trade and labour standards. To say a few words about trade and the environment since it is one area in which GATT member countries have committed themselves already to a comprehensive new work programme. They decided on 15 December, in conjunction with the adoption of the results of the Uruguay Round negotiations, to draw up a work programme on trade and environment by the Ministerial meeting in Marrakesh. Environmental policy-making is one of the most rapidly evolving areas of national and international policy-making, and it is entirely appropriate that emphasis should be placed now in GATT/WTO on ensuring better policy coordination and multilateral cooperation over the linkages between trade and environment.

Permanent Negotiations

The Uruguay Round may well be the last of its kind, but this in no way means the end of multilateral trade negotiations. On the contrary, it means they become a permanent event. Ad hoc negotiating rounds were necessary mainly because the GATT lacked the mandate or the institutional basis to operate the multilateral system to the full on a continuous basis. Between rounds the GATT has tended to lose momentum, often at the very times when it was essential to make the most of the liberalising impulse. This has allowed protectionism and unilateralism to recover and regroup and meant that each round has to start by regaining lost ground.

The positive results of the Uruguay Round will redefine much more than assumptions about trade. If they are exploited with the same determination, courage and commitment that went into concluding the Round, they should mean nothing less than a new start for sustainable growth and a new system of collective economic security for the world.

But if the trading system is now up to the job of supporting multilateral cooperation on such a wide scale, do the other structures of economic cooperation still meet the bill? The establishment of the WTO will put trade and investment on a par—perhaps rather in advance—of cooperation in monetary and financial areas. The WTO will stand alongside its original Bretton Woods sisters, the IMF and the World Bank. The three institutions must learn to work together even more effectively and closely. For example, rather than each body conducting separate reviews of country policies, is there not a case to be made for a more integrated approach on country reviews? But that does not, on its own, add up to effective multilateral economic cooperation. The question really has to be asked seriously: are the G7, the OECD, the regional groupings adequate to provide that cooperation?

It is the next challenge of international economic leadership—the challenge of translating the common interest in global growth into a practical and effective mechanism for solving our common economic problems together. So, the Ministers meeting in Marrakesh is an historic event which will establish the World Trade Organisation and put in place the new multilateral trading system, they will be making not an end, but a beginning.

❊ ❊ ❊

2

Export Subsidies

A Distortion to Free Trade in Agriculture

Export subsidies are generally considered one of the most distorting trade tools used by governments to interfere with commercial markets. Export subsidies allow a government to determine the level and direction of trade solely on the basis of government subsidies, lowering world prices and denying sales for other, more competitive exporters. Not only are export subsidies unfair commercial tools, but, by encouraging surplus production, they encourage adverse environmental practices, waste government budgets, and may delay restructuring and reform of domestic industries. Substantial progress toward eliminating export subsidies will be a critical element of the World Trade Organisation (WTO) negotiations scheduled to begin at the end of this year.

The Situation Today

Under the Uruguay Round Agreement, countries agreed to strictly limit the use of export subsidies. First, products that had not benefited from export subsidies in the past were banned from receiving them in the future. Second, where countries had provided export subsidies in the past, their future use was capped and gradually reduced over 6 to 10 years. Developed countries were required to cut their spending on export subsidies by 36 per cent over six years while also reducing subsidised export quantities by at least 21 per cent on a commodity-specific basis.

Developing countries have until 2005 to cut spending by 24 per cent and subsidised quantities by 14 per cent. Third, countries agreed not to create new schemes that serve as disguised subsidies to get around the product-specific limits. Finally, countries recognised that export credit and food aid programmes were different and exempted them from the new budget and quantity limits, although there was agreement to negotiate disciplines on export credit programmes to ensure that they do not undermine WTO commitments.

Today, the European Union (EU) is the primary export subsidiser—accounting for nearly 85 per cent of the world total. Nearly all other countries agreed in the last round of negotiations not to use or to have only limited recourse to use export subsidies. EU farmers, responding to domestic prices that are often twice the world price, produce more products than can be consumed in Europe, but at such high prices that they can be sold abroad only with generous subsidies. These subsidies force other competitors out of the market and discourage production in countries with comparative advantage.

If the EU's extravagant domestic subsidies are the root cause of export subsidies, they are also putting serious pressure on the whole EU system. The need to impose budgetary discipline on EU farm programmes (annual cost, about $46 billion) is becoming increasingly evident, even in Europe, and the EU's goal of expanding its membership to new countries is putting pressure on it to bring its farm programmes into line with other countries, which will help reduce its need to rely on export subsidies in the future.

Areas for Resolution

The upcoming negotiations should continue the work begun in the Uruguay Round and eliminate existing export subsidies. There is no economic justification for their continued use. By removing subsidised exports, world prices should increase, and farmers, particularly in the EU, will not be artificially encouraged to overproduce products that they cannot grow competitively.

In addition to eliminating export subsidies, countries should examine the rules defining export subsidies to ensure that countries do not resort to other policy tools that might allow governments to distort markets. Specially, WTO members should to look closely at curbing agricultural state trading export monopolies that can exert undue market power or dispose of surplus commodies on a non-market basis. A recent WTO victory by the United States and New Zealand over Canada's special-class system of dairy exports shows that the existing rule against circumvention are effective but must be enforced.

Export credit and food aid programmes were addressed in the Uruguay Round agreement in recognition of the fact that those tools could be disguised as subsidies. These policies may again be on the agenda when the WTO negotiations commence next time. It will be important to ensure that the world's needy continue to have access to imported products, even when financial turmoil rolls would markets and limits the ability of developing countries to meet their food and fiber needs.

Certain large exporting nations—primarily in the EU have used export taxes as a supply management tool by intervening in the market to restrict exports when domestic stocks are low. These measures can wreak havoc in international markets, exacerbating price swings and reducing the confidence of net-food-importing countries to abandon trade barriers and rely on the international market to provide food security. Similarly, some exporting countries use differential export taxes to discourage exports of basic products (such as grains or oilseeds); they force exporters to process the product domestically (into flour or oil and meal, for example) and export the value added products.

***

3

International Trade with the Consumer's Money

When trade policies are discussed nationally or internationally people as consumers are largely forgotten. Despite their numbers, they do not carry the weight that producers and other lobbies command. Individually, consumers are seldom informed about how the availability, quality, price and choice of the hundreds of items which they buy in the shops each year are affected by trade policy decisions. If they know-how much of their household budgets are determined by decisions to protect individual industries and for how little effect they might be shocked.

Equally, when it is debated publicly, the benefits that would fall to the consumers are usually ignored. This brief study is an attempt to put the consumer interest squarely in the public arena.

How Do Government Decisions on Trade Affect the Consumer?

Virtually all protective policies mean higher prices for the consumer. And if it is not a consumer who pays, it will be domestic producer. These are some of the main actions taken by national authorities.

Governments frequently and for the most part, legally raise revenue and protect domestic industries by imposing duties on imported products. If a product has a 25 per cent tariff, the price in the shop will normally be 25 per cent more than its price at the port or airport.

Global quotas and other numerical limits on imports are sometimes legal sometimes not. Either way the intention is to restrict access to the market in such a away that domestic producers of the same product can raise their prices without being forced out of business through lack of competitiveness. Quotas are frequently preferred by those demanding protection because the impact on prices is less obvious than with a tariff. Once again, prices go up in the shops and limits may be so narrow that goods disappear from the shelves altogether.

Voluntary export restraints are quotas of an even more costly kind for the importing country. They allow foreign suppliers to charge higher prices than would be possible under a tariff or normal quota. By "bribing" the exporter this way, opposition to the protection is reduced.

Subsidies are sometimes paid to domestic producers to help them compete with import competition by keeping their costs artificially low. This keeps prices down. Unfortunately, the consumer as a tax payer ends up paying for the subsidy. In so doing, he is prevented from keeping more of his income to spend on other goods, which may be produced by more efficient industries. One thing is sure once industries get used to subsidies, it is very hard to wean then away.

Rules permit governments to impose extra duties on imports where products are shown to be dumped (sold below the normal price in the exporting country) or subsidised, and where the effect of dumping or subsidisation is demonstrated to damage the corresponding domestic industry. While these duties may be justified, they nevertheless always serve to raise the price for consumers to knock products completely out of the market. Yet very few, if any, countries give much weight to consumer interest when deciding whether to impose such penalty duties. And their use had grown disturbingly in recent years.

Governments usually impose standards of safety, quality, public health and environmental protection for good reasons often in the interests of consumers. Sometimes, however, the standards and the procedures which enforce them are no more than hidden protection for domestic producers. In imposing unnecessary measures on imports, governments penalize consumers through higher prices and the non-availability of goods.

Protection tends to be loaded towards the products which are essentials for any family. Consequently, since the essential command the biggest proportion of the household budgets of poor families, protection acts as a regressive tax.

Clothing is a good example. The multifibre arrangement acts on low-cost products, raising prices and restricting availability, meanwhile up-market goods are seldom affected. Moreover, for the poor consumer, the effect is further exaggerated. Foreign producers will tend to export higher quality end, therefore, more expensive goods, in order to maximise their profits from the quota. This quality upgrading effect not only reduces disproportionately the supply of lower-priced clothing, but may also affect the supply of children's clothing.

Consumers have enjoyed an enormous growth in the range and quality of products in their shops as a result of the multilateral training system. Many fruit and vegetables are available even out of season throughout the year. Exotic foods, never seen just ten or twenty years ago, are now commonly found on super-market selves. Cut flowers are being transported fresh by cargo plane daily from one country to the other. The range and sophistication of domestic electronic products would have been unimaginable had their development not been spurred by the availability of a global market.

Household Costs are Not the Only Consumer Cost Which Go Up

Many industries are also consumers of imported goods. Manufacturers can depend on cheaper and better products from overseas in order to maintain their own competitiveness in their domestic market and, especially, in their export markets.

The best example is steel. Many companies require either specialty steel or basic steel products at the lowest possible prices. Unfortunately, because of export restraints, formal quotas, anti-dumping and countervailing duties and high tariffs. Sometimes they cannot even find the precise type or quality of steel they need. They are, therefore, put at a huge competitive disadvantage.

Semiconductors and other electronic components are also subject to this self-defeating form of protection. Just as the price of steel puts up the price of automobiles, so high tariffs, anti-dumping duties and quotas on electronic components puts up the prices of video recorders, personal computers and other advanced consumer electronic products. Meanwhile foreign competitors continue to buy their semi-conductor inputs at world market prices.

But is One of the Prices a Lowering of Public Health and Safety Standards?

It has been suggested that some measures to ensure safe good for consumers and to prevent the spread of pests of diseases among animals and plants do not amount to unjustified barriers to trade.

The first point is that if there is some justification for them, these measures—even if they restrict trade—are completely permissible. The main objective is to make them transparent, to discourage arbitrary decision-making and discrimination and to minimise any restriction on trade.

The second point is that would encourage governments to establish measures consistent with international standards and guidelines. This is important because it could mean a general raising of standards: in many areas even advanced industrial countries do not meet international standards on food safety.

Third, the governments has to impose more stringent standards than those agreed internationally. The only condition is that a government so doing might, if challenged, be required to show scientific evidence or some kind of risk assessment to support the measure.

It should also be noted that with the reduction of agricultural subsidies which encourage unlimited production (those supporting farmers' income directly will still be permitted) consumers should see more products produced by less chemical intensive farming methods in the shops.

❋ ❋ ❋

4

Add Value, Go Global

Can Southern Firms Break into Export Markets?

The global economy has changed beyond recognition over the last decade. Widespread economic policy reform and in particular trade liberalisation have opened up new opportunities for developing countries. In poor countries, however, the consequences of trade liberalisation are not always positive. What can the private sector do to respond better and make the most of new trading opportunities? What factors have limited the impact of economic reforms on export performance?

Why have exports from poorer countries failed to increase more rapidly following trade liberalisation? What can be done to improve performance? Research on the response of firms in the private sector to economic reform can underpin new approaches to export promotion for poorer developing countries. For a long time, protective trade policies, poorly performing state-owned industries and state controls over the private sector were blamed for poor export performance in Africa and South Asia. Now that some of these problems have been remedied, other obstacles have come to light.

The effect of economic liberalisation and adjustment on the performance of poor countries has been cause for concern. Trade liberalisation should increase incentives to export and facilitate business enterprise by encouraging private ownership through privatisation and by attracting foreign investment. Macroeconomic stability ought to boost business confidence and performance. All these factors should promote exports, offsetting job and income losses caused by the closure or reorganisation of inefficient enterprises and industries yet, although some degree of reform and stability it is without export growth that was expected.

Trade reform and macroeconomic stability may be necessary conditions for improved export performance put by them are insufficient. The obstacles to improving export performance are numerous and there is no easy policy answer. The research programme examined export performance at three levels.

- **Regional:** How trade strategies should vary with skills and natural resource endowments
- **National:** Factors influencing the export performance of manufacturing
- **Sectoral:** The performance of particular sectors of the economy.

The East Asian economies have shown that developing countries can compete successfully in global markets. For many, they provide a blueprint for economic growth applicable to many poor countries.

South Asia's comparative advantage lies in its abundant unskilled labour, while Africa's lies in its abundant natural resources. Different export promotion strategies are essential. South Asia's best prospects are in labour-intensive manufacturing: the region's low level of exports would soar over the next decade if current obstacles to trade were reduced. Africa's exports could also increase but its biggest potential in primary products that need little educated labour and abundant natural resources.

Some African countries could also be substantial exporters of manufacturers, but their actual manufactured exports in most cases now fall far short. Comparing Ghana to Mauritius—one of Africa's most successful exporters of manufactured goods differences in firm-level efficiency are apparent Mauritian firms have more capital per worker and use it more efficiently. Reducing trade barriers is not sufficient. Wages in Ghana would have to be substantially lower to offset low labour productivity. Alternatively, labour productivity will have to be drastically improved if Ghanian firms are to compete successfully in export markets with wages at current levels.

Even when companies use capital and labour efficiently, poor infrastructure is a frequent stumbling products to export markets—an acute problem in landlocked countries and equally acute for manufacturers as research on Uganda clearly shows. What huts manufacturing exporters is being hit by the high cost of transporting their output to foreign markets and of transporting the materials they need from abroad. The cost penalties resulting from geography and poor infrastructure are far greater in Uganda than from high tariffs and other import restrictions.

Southern firms can still break into export markets, however, developing—country firms do export to markets with exacting standards for product quality, reliability of delivery, and consumer safety. Two crucial aspects, however, are often overlooked:

- Non-manufacturing sectors, such as tourism and horticulture, generate significant employment and offer opportunities for supplying increasingly sophisticated products. Although manufacturing is considered more attractive, certain areas of tourism and horticulture can be equally appealing.
- New export opportunities are created as southern producers establish closer links with foreign customers. Producers of labour-intensive products such as garments, horticulture and footwear frequently depend on large retailers and specialist international traders for designs, information about demand and technical support.

Supermarkets make key decisions about which fruits and vegetables to grow, how they should be produced and processed and which firms should be included in the business.

Strategic decisions by international producers and retailers in the footwear industry have been crucial in developing new production locations such as Vietnam and Romania. Similarly, work on automotive components production in South Africa and India illustrates how global sourcing by the leading motor companies closes off some markets and opens up others. Export prospects can only be evaluated in the light of global restructuring in these industries.

Emphasising global linkages does not mean that developing countries are powerless in the face of global forces. Even in tightly-structured industries, there is scope for national policy and national strategy. Furthermore, there are important export sectors that are not structured in this way. Some tourism is dominated by large northern firms and is heavily import-dependent, but there is also enormous potential and national policy will be crucial in shaping the industry and its contribution to the economy as a whole.

For southern firms to break into export markets, certain issues must be addressed, especially in Africa. Some are recognised as important policy issues—investing in human capital and improving infrastructure for example. As one set of constraints are reduced—such as removing policy—induced distortions through trade liberalisation—another set takes precedence. In response to the integration of global markets, southern producers must join the global distribution chains to ensure markets for their exports.

These findings impose hard choices on developing countries. Should a firm allocate limited funds for investment in human capital or investment infrastructure? Future research might contribute by quantifying relative rates of return. On another level, countries may worry about the independence and autonomy of local producers if they are to join a global chain typically donated by northern companies. Rules regulate governmental trade and investment policies but who controls the global buyers and multinational companies whose decisions have such huge impacts on developing countries?

❋ ❋ ❋

5

Market Access
Eliminating Barriers that Impede Trade

Market access for particular commodities continues to be restricted by high tariffs and tariff-rate quotas (TRQs). The administration of TRQ systems in different countries can impede and distort commercial decision-making. One of the most important accomplishments of the Uruguay Round agreement was bringing agriculture more fully under General Agreement on Tariffs and Trade disciplines. A principal implication of this is that trade in agricultural products can now be restricted only by tariffs—quotas, discriminatory licensing, and other non-tariff measures are forbidden. Also, all agricultural tariffs were "bound" In the World Trade Organization (WTO); tariff rates above a binding violate WTO obligations.

While creating a "tariff-only" system for agricultural products is an important advance, too many market access barriers continue to impede international trade of food and fiber products. Market access barriers deny efficient producers the opportunity to compete in other markets and limit the variety and quality of products available to consumers. Reducing and removing these barriers will be an important element of the WTO negotiations.

What are the Issues?

Eliminating non-tariff measurers was a necessary first step to removing trade barriers, but many of the tariffs in place are still prohibitively high. For example, while the average tariff assessed by the United States on agricultural products is less than 5 per cent (and for industrial products is less than 5 per cent (and for industrial products is nearly zero), the average agricultural tariff assessed by WTO members exceeds 50 per cent.

Moreover, in some cases, market access for a particular product is restricted to a Tariff-Rate Quota (TRQ). Under a TRQ system, import opportunities are established for a specific quantity of imports at a low tariff. All other imports of a product are subject to high tariffs. All tariffs, including in-quota and out of quota tariffs, are now bound against increase and subject to further reductions, a situation that will be a top priority in the next round of negotiations.

Where TRQs remain as a transitional step before more open trade is achieved, further reform needs to be undertaken in the upcoming negotiations. In the Uruguay Round, countries generally agreed to open TRQs to allow imports equal to current levels of trade or, where imports had been low, new access opportunities were established. Recent experience also indicates that the administration of the TRQ systems in different countries can impede trade and distort commercial decision-making. It is expected that these elements will be subject to further disciplines in the upcoming negotiations.

Similarly, we need to closely examine the rules for state trading import monopolies in agriculture. Use of these state traders may have been justifiable when more restrictions were allowed on farm trade, but in the tariff only regime, it is difficult to see why a government needs to insert itself between thrust of WTO principles, countries should use the upcoming negotiations to increase responses to market forces competition and transparency where single-desk buyers or other restrictions on the right to import exist.

Although the WTO has moved agriculture to a tariff—only system, in too many cases countries operate variable tariff systems that result in confusing and unpredictable tariff collection. Measures such as reference-price schemes, price-brand systems, and variable tariffs operating under a high WTO binding make it hard for businesses to know exactly what tariff they will have to pay when their product arrives at customs. The uncertainty and lack of transparency chills trade and leaves the system open to potential fraud and abuse. In some cases, reference-price systems can disadvantage suppliers of products with particular grades or quality. Countries are likely to investigate the operation of such tariff systems in the upcoming negotiations.

One of the elements of the Uruguay Round agreement was to establish a special agricultural safeguard mechanism to protect particularly sensitive products against a flood of imports or to guard against a sudden drop in the price of imports. The agreement establishes specific criteria for triggering the safeguard mechanism. Countries are expected to review the operation of the safeguard and review whether to continue its use in the upcoming negotiations.

❋❋❋

6

Trading Towards Peace

The reason why trade has such a vital part to play in building peace is because it means lowering barriers—not only to goods and services but among nations and peoples. The elimination of barriers creates interdependence and interdependence creates solidarity. The history of the last fifty years has shown us all the undeniable benefits of lowering trade barriers and opening economies.

Clearly every region has its own characteristics, and it would be wrong to imagine that the same blueprint can apply everywhere and in the same way. Any region which was for thousands of years at the crosswords of world trade should regain its place in the centre, because doing so will help build peace as well as prosperity. This is why the numerous applications for accession to the WTO from various countries are so significant. The first is through regionalism. There are several efforts at regional trade and economic initiatives among countries, and that such initiatives will be encouraged to reduce positive results. Regional initiatives are important because they can help countries at a comparable level of development to move relatively quickly in opening their economies and in deepening their interdependence.

However, the rapid advance of global economic integration means that while regional initiatives remain important, they are not sufficient by themselves to address successfully the new perspectives of the international economy. That is why there is a need for second track, which is the rule-based multilateral system. And that is why the multilateral system is of fundamental importance to the economic prosperity of any region.

As the first major international institution to be created in the post-Cold War era, the WTO offers a promise of the kind of global economic architecture which need in the coming decades. Its culture is firmly rooted in the tradition of consensus-building and coopeation among sovereign countries. And the WTO embodies rights and obligations negotiated by consensus, approved and ratified by each government and each parliament, and they are enforceable, not through the crude exercise of economic power, but through the rule of law. The alternative would be a power-based system—who would want to chose this option?

But most importantly the WTO is an organisation which brings all countries—from all corners of the world and from all levels of development—together as equals. There is no weighted voting, no exclusive clubs, no inner and outer circles. Developing countries representing 80 per cent of constituency sit as equals with industrialised countries to write the rules of a shared trading system.

This new unity of developing and developed countries inside a single system will be credited as the greatest achievement of the multilateral system. But this unity is still fragile: we cannot allow it to be broken: This is why, in preparing the agenda of the first Ministerial meeting in Singapore, have recognised the particularly difficult task facing developing countries in implementing the Uruguay Round Commitments. They have also acknowledged the challenges they face in contemplating the necessary work programme.

The integration of developing countries as equal partners in the multilateral system is one of the most important challenges in shaping the economic order of the 21st century. This is a shared responsibility of developed and developing countries alike. There is no rational alternative to this objective. The evolution of the global economy makes that clear.

Now there is a need to work together as equal partners to ensure the full integration, and all other developing and transition economies, into the global economy and the rule-based multilateral trading system. In conjunction with this there is a need to encourage, notably with growth of regional economic cooperation. The alternative is a vicious circle where economic isolation feeds greater political instability which in turn leads to greater economic isolation. The road to a lasting peace in the world begins, not ends, with economic integration and interdependence. Taking this message to heart will help build a future where it is goods, services, and investment that cross borders—not missiles and soldiers.

❋❋❋

7

Free Trade as Peacemaker

The Benefits of an Open World Trading System

Globalisation by free trade according to the principles of the World Trade Organisation (WTO) offers the only realistic opportunity to integrate the world peacefully and in time to prevent a major disaster. The primacy of the economy over politics is the most important vehicle for a successful world domestic policy.

Since Adam Smith, traditional economic theory has on principle been well-disposed towards free trade. Free trade enables better use of the world's economic resources than does national protectionism. Countries can concentrate on their respective strength and draw from their trade partners the goods they need, but do not produce. But there have always been objections against free trade.

The international trade system has always been encumbered by disperate accusations of unfair competition. The fear that foreign competitors use unfair methods, such as dumping, as and is widespread. If one were to believe all the charges of dumping that are made, then international trade would have been completely destroyed long ago. Great restraint should be exercised with respect to allegations of dumping if one is interested in maintaining an interweaving of international economic activities.

The Free Trade Opposition Cloaks Itself in Dumping Charges

The modern form of the struggle against free trade

cloaks itself in the accusation of ecological dumping or social dumping. With this difficult subject matter, one should not make sweeping generalisations. These things also are not gone into in detail in what follows.

Environmental protection is an asset that every economy produces at the cost of other assets. The people's preferences for the asset of environmental protection probably varies from country to country. It is also completely legitimate and does not at all distort trade if the environmental provisions—in line with the different national preferences—vary from country to country.

In the rich Western European economic region, one should guard against a new form of cultural imperialism. It is not for this part of the world to impose its preferences for environmental assets on other countries, especially Third World countries. Free world trade brings not only economic advantages. Even more important is its contribution to lasting world peace.

In view of world population growth, every standstill in the movement towards a peaceful world society must be seen as a step backwards. We are compelled to run a race between the growing problems and the development of stable institutions to overcome them peacefully at global level. Economic history since the end of the World War II shows clearly that free trade under the old GATT was of decisive importance for the prosperity of the industrialised nations.

The principle of help for self-help has nowhere been applied so consistently as on the free world market. In reverse, the examples of countries that cut themselves off from the world market show the disastrous consequences of the rigidity of a society which shuns the pressure of international competition.

Revolutionary Success of Open-Market Policies

The West's policy of open markets pursued since 1948 and reinforced since 1989 has led to a dynamism which, in the true meaning of the word, is revolutionary. More than half the world population now lives in countries with annual GDP growth rates of more than 5 per cent. Europe is not among that group, which may be why it also stands somewhat apart in its mentality.

Certainly, there also can be undesirable trends in free trade. There is no ideal systems; one must choose between imperfect potentialities. However, no realistically better substitute for the free trade system is in sight, not even with respect to the goals of a pacified world: an ecological sound world economy and a balance of global dimensions between the poor and the rich. An ideal government of philosopher kings armed with absolute power certainly could do something better than does free trade—but such a government remains fictitious. There are tangible and narrow limits to what the political system, whether democratic or not, can effect in a positive sense. This is how the structural conservatism of democratic and other political systems impedes the timely assertion of reforms necessary to achieve a world peace society.

The GATT was turned into the World Trade Organisation (WTO) a few years ago. Besides extending the free trade principle to services and additional agricultural sectors, the new agreement foresees above all the full inclusion of the Third World in the system. The agreement commits the industrialised nations to open their markets to developing and threshold countries.

Other important points are the strengthening and tightening of the dispute mediation process. Based on a system of relatively independent *ad hoc* panels, it permits complaints against WTO member countries for violations of the agreement. Thus, what is arising here is an effective global jurisdiction within the meaning of a peaceful world domestic policy.

Exclusion as Penalty

The decisive sanction mechanism of the WTO—which

is not a specialist organisation of the United Nations—is the threat of exclusion. Exclusion would deny the penalised country free access to the markets of WTO members on the basis of most favoured nation status. This is a threat that requires no armed force, but is very effective. No country can still afford to do without the beneficial effects on prosperity that participation in international trade brings.

Thus, with the threat of denial of access to world markets for violating WTO rules, and the guarantee of a more or less fair competition for a country's own products for abiding by them, a non-military sanctions system has come into being. That is substantial progress on the path to a pacified world.

Certainly, this sanction system's sphere of influence is limited for the time being. Essentially, it will be used to assert the game rules of free trade. It offers no legal grounds for pressing other goals, such as on human rights. Attempting to expand it in this direction would for the foreseeable future put the entire system at risk.

In the current debate on globalisation, the question arises of whether the world economic institutions should not be converted in this manner, that politics regains its autonomy, and that the primacy of politics can be restored. The critics of globalisation point to the constraints to adjust which the world economy exercises on national or continental politics. However well this demand for the primacy of politics may be justified in philosophical terms, it virtually comes down to a demand for the ascendancy of the conservative principle.

Danger of a Slowed-Down World Integration

The demand for the primacy of politics is gaining strength from the desire to avoid the pressure to adjust which the dynamics of world events are exerting. It is today a conservative, and in fact a reactionary, longing for the (Utopian) return of the functioning European welfare state of two or three decades ago. If it were asserted, it would mean practically slowing-down world integration. It would run dead against the goal of a world policy based on a desire for peace.

The present primacy of the economy over politics—in terms of the free movement of goods, services and capital—is basically nothing more than the priority of the global principle over the provincial, the national principle. As such, it gives the principle of change pre-eminence over the principle of maintaining the status quo. What gives the primacy of the economy its legitimacy? Probably not the thought that world peace better be secured by this means. Its legitimation lies in the very indirect economic success that the free trade system delivers. For the reflective observer, the question remains of whether this legitimation is sufficient.

To answer this question, however, and particularly if one pleads for maintaining the ascendancy of the economy, it appears appropriate to outline the consequences that can be expected from further integration of the world economy. As can be seen today in East and Southeast Asia, the growth dynamics of the world economy will lead to a marked rise in the living standards of a large part of the Third World.

Do not Exclude Poor Countries from the Competition

The global consequences of Asia's growth should not have been seen only negatively. While it also may mean, for example, a great burden on the global climate, it leads at the same time to an acceleration of the process of falling birth rates and thus to an earlier stabilisation of the world population. Prosperity for the Third World is so far the only realistic answer to the urgent problem of population growth. And free competition on the world market in the only reliable means of achieving this prosperity in the course of some decades.

Despite ecological sacrifice in the medium term, continuation of Third World growth is the only way to solve the long-term ecological problems. One also should not forget that only those who can eat their fill and have a roof over their heads are prepared to reflect on ecology and discuss it.

As for the rest, the balance between rich and poor is more acceptable when the poor become richer than when the rich become poorer. That applies also at the international level. The market and access to it are peaceful sanctions of the world economic system on the basis of free trade. Those who are hungry and have nothing more to lose are more of a danger to world peace than those who have eaten their fill. The ruse of covering up domestic problems by cross-border military aggression will become less attractive to the degree that a country's own economy is integrated in the global economic system. The more countries are economically dependent on each other, the more unlikely it is that they will wage war on each other.

Globalisation by free trade according to the principles of the WTO offers the only realistic opportunity to integrate the world peacefully and in time to prevent a major disaster. The primacy of the economy is the most important vehicle for a successful world domestic policy.

8

The WTO and the Developing Countries

The special status of developing countries in the GATT will continue to receive recognition in the WTO. The preamble of the Agreement establishing the WTO states that "there is a need for positive efforts designed to ensure that developing countries, and especially the least developed among them, secure a share in the growth of international trade commensurate with the needs of their economic development". In addition to retaining the provisions that concerned developing countries in GATT 1947, the new agreement generally contain provisions for developing countries and least-developed countries, often consisting of longer transition periods for the full implementation of some obligations and various exemptions from obligations, particularly for the latter group of countries. Also, in some instances, the exports of developing countries benefit from a better treatment with respect to measures taken by other WTO members. Technical assistance is to be provided to developing countries to assist them in assuming their obligations and more effectively realising the benefits of the multilateral trading system.

Least-developed countries are singled out in the Final Act as requiring special attention. This is reflected in the Agreements through a number of provisions which provide the most favourable treatment for this group in terms of rights as well as lower levels of obligations. In addition, the Decision on Measures in Favour of Least-Developed Countries, makes provision for measures of special assistance, including technical assistance "in the development, strengthening and diversification of their production and export bases including those of services, as well as in trade promotion, to enable them to maximise the benefits from liberalised access to markets". As part of its functions, the Committee on Trade and Development (a subsidiary body of the General Council) will periodically review the special provisions in favour of least-developed countries and report to the General Council of the WTO for appropriate action.

The Declaration on the Contribution of the WTO to Achieving Greater Coherence in Global Economic Policy making identifies the need for strengthening the relationship between the activities of the WTO, the International Monetary Fund (IMF) and the World Bank as a way of ensuring greater coherence in global economic policy-making.

Market Access

Industrial Products: For developed countries, the main features of their market access commitments in industrial products include the expansion of bindings to cover 99 per cent of imports; the expansion of duty free access from 30 to 44 per cent of total imports; and the reduction of the trade-weighted average tariff by 40 per cent (i.e. from the per-Uruguay Round level of 6.2 per cent to the post-Uruguay Round level of 3.7 per cent). With respect to tariff reductions on individual product categories, developed countries will reduce tariffs by substantially above-average amounts (60 per cent or more) in three categories—wood, pulp, paper and furniture; metals; and non-electric machinery and reduce tariffs by less than the 40 per cent overall reduction in four categories—fish and fish products; textiles and clothing; leather, rubber, footwear and transport equipment.

In terms of exports from developing to developed country markets, the total reduction in the average tariff of developed countries is 37 per cent. Below average tariff reductions, and above average levels of tariffs apply to labour-intensive manufacturers (textiles and clothing, leather goods) and certain processed primary products (fish products) that have been—and continue to be—regarded as "sensitive".

Developed countries constitute the most important merchandise exports markets for developing countries (62 per cent in 1992). In part, this is because the developed countries account for the bulk of global income and expenditures. At the same time, market access opportunities for developing countries in each other's markets have long been affected by the protection in their own markets. In many instances, the level of protection is quite high, because important protection, ultimately, acts as a tax on exports as well, protection in developing countries also hinders the integration of developing countries also hinders the integration of developing economies, not just with each other, but with the larger global trading system.

The reductions in bound tariffs which the new commitments of developing economies represent are difficult to assess for several reasons. The first is that comprehensive information on base (1986) tariffs is unavailable in many cases as a result of the low level of bindings among developing countries. In these cases, the post-Uruguay Round average bound tariff usually involves a decrease in the ceiling bindings applied to items already found, combined with ceiling bindings above currently applied rates for previously unbound items. Another reason is that, where developing economies had bound all or a significant portion of tariffs prior to the end of the Round, the Uruguay Round tariff commitments often reflect a decline in ceiling rates (rather than applied rates).

At the same time, current tariff levels already reflect the often substantial reductions undertaken autonomously in the course of the Round. Though many developing countries may not be required to introduce further cuts, previous liberalisation has been at least partly locked in through new commitments on bindings. Ceiling bindings are considered to be so important that countries which agree to bind previously unbound tariffs are given "negotiating credits" for the decision even if the tariff is bound at a level above the currently applied level (as is the case for many developing economy participants in the Round). Bindings have also played a key role in establishing the domestic and international credibility of domestic reform programmes in many countries. Although an integral part of the tariff negotiations, bindings clearly are more akin to rules and procedures—in terms of their contribution to the predictability of future market access—than to direct increases in market access. However, even ceiling bindings yield significant benefits related to liberalisation when they reduce the expect value and variance of protection.

On the basis of data available for 26 developing countries, the GATT Secretariat has identified the main features of their market access commitments. These include: the expansion of bindings to cover 61 per cent of imports, compared to the pre-Uruguay Round level of 13 per cent. The increase in the security of trade among developing regions is reflected mainly in Latin America—where participants will bind 100 per cent of tariff lines at ceilings rates.

Too often, "market access" as used in descriptions of the Uruguay Round results is defined—implicitly or explicitly in a way that is too narrow and, even worse, mercantilist. The narrowness results from limiting the analysis of changes in market access to changes in tariffs and quotas. This overlooks three other key aspects of market access, namely the bindings of tariffs, the rules and disciplines on the use of other trade-related government interventions, and the institutional arrangements for monitoring and enforcing compliance with those disciplines. It is progress in these latter three areas that determines the security of increases in market access from reductions in tariffs and the elimination of quantitative restrictions. Since the gains from trade liberalisation depend heavily on the stimulus it provides to trade-related investment, the security aspect is crucial.

Agricultural Products: Increased market access for agricultural products includes the "tariffication" of all non-tariff border measures (conversion to tariff-equivalents)—with the exception of those products for which special treatment has been negotiated—and a binding of all tariffs on agricultural products. As a result, the security of trade in agricultural products will for the first time be greater than in industrial products, since 100 per cent of agricultural product tariff lines will be bound.

Tariffs resulting from the "tariffication" process, together with the other tariffs on agricultural products, are to be reduced by a simple average of 36 per cent over six years in the case of developed countries and 24 per cent over ten years in the case of developing countries, with minimum reductions per tariff line of 15 per cent and 10 per cent, respectively. The reductions in the tariffs of developed countries—which account for about two-thirds of world imports of agricultural products—indicate an average percentage reduction of 37 per cent. With respect to individual product categories, developed countries will cut tariffs by above—average amounts on oilseeds, flowers an plants; and cut tariffs by below—average amounts on sugar and dairy products, with other product categories close to the average cut. In the categories of "topical products", which account for half of exports of developing countries of agricultural products, a 43 per cent reduction in tariffs will be implemented by developed countries.

Current access opportunities will be maintained on terms at least equivalent to those existing prior to the tariffication process. However, for those products where tariffication took place and imports were less than 5 per cent of domestic consumption because of the existing restrictions, minimum market access commitments, implemented through tariff quotas on an MFN basis at a low or minimal tariff rate, are required. Figures on the increased market access in terms of tonnage resulting from minimum access commitments indicate that substantial increases in market access occur for coarse grains (1,757,000 tons) and rice

(1,076,000 tons), as well as for other products. With regard to commitments on export competition, the quantities of exports which can be legally subsidised must be reduced by 21 per cent. Furthermore, total export subsidy outlays will decline by 36 per cent, from $21.3 billion to $13.7 billion by the end of the transition period. The importance of this commitment is that, on average, developed countries subsidised annually during 1986-90, 48.2 million tons of wheat, 19.5 million tons of coarse grains, 1.8 million tons of sugar, 1.2 million tons of beef, etc. With regard to commitments on domestic support to agricultural producers, total outlays (in terms of the Aggregate Measurement of Support) will be reduced by 18 per cent, from $197, billion to $162 billion by the end of the transition period.

The new market access opportunities for agricultural products which will result from the Uruguay Round—as a result of a change in border measures, and policies relating to export competition and domestic support—will be of particular interest to developing countries exporting temperature food products. More generally, multilateral discipliners on trade-distorting practices in agriculture are expected to stabilise world food markets in the coming decades, providing potential trade opportunities for developing countries and reducing fluctuations in food import bills. However, the potential situation in net food-importing developing countries is of particular concern. Potential problems relating to least-developed and net food importing developing countries are the subject of the Decision on *Measures Concerning the Possible Negative Effects of the Reform Programme on Least-Developed and Net Food Importing Developing Countries*. The decision sets out objectives with regard to the provision of food aid, the provision of basic foodstuffs in full grant form and aid for agricultural development. It also refers to the possibility of assistance from the International Monetary Fund and the World Bank with respect to the short-term financing of food imports. The WTO Committee of Agriculture will monitor the implementation of the decision.

WTO Agreements Covering Trade in Goods

GATT 1994: The cornerstone of trade relations in the area of goods. Differential and more favourable treatment to developing countries and to least-developed countries is permitted under the 1979 Enabling Clause with respect to tariffs in the context of the Generalised System of Preferences (GSP) and non-tariff measures, notwithstanding the most-favoured-nation clause, and with respect to regional or global arrangements concluded by developing countries.

Agreements Integrating Practices Otherwise on the Margin of GATT Rules: Includes Trade Related Investment Measures (TRIMs) (which can be found to be inconsistent with the national treatment provision or the prohibition on quantitative restrictions), such as local content requirements or trade-balancing requirements. GATT inconsistent TRIMs are required to be notified and eliminated within a transition period of and two years (developed countries), five years (developing countries) or seven years (least-developed countries). A further extension may be requested by developing and least-developed countries. The Agreement on Safeguards prohibits the use of "grey-area measures", such as voluntary restraints or orderly marketing arrangements; such measures are to be notified and eliminated.

Agreement on Textiles and Clothing: Provides for the eventual elimination of the Multi-Fibre Arrangement (MFA) after a ten-year transition period. In place since 1973, the MFA currently groups eight "importers"; of these, Austria, Canada, the European Communities, Finland, Norway and the United States apply restrictions under the MFA, while Japan and Switzerland do not. The other participants in the MFA are the "exporters" (mainly developing countries), whose exports or part of their exports covered by the MFA are subject to bilaterally agreed quantitative restraints or unilaterally imposed restraints on imports, typically applied at the product level but in some cases to various aggregates as wells.

Trade in Services

The General Agreement on Trade in Services (GATS) is the first multilateral agreement on trade that has its objective the progressive liberalisation of trade in services. It provide for secure and more open market in services in a similar manner as the GATT has done for trade in goods. The Agreement covers trade in all service sectors and the supply of service in all forms.

The GATS has two components: the framework agreement containing 29 Articles and a number of Annexes, Ministerial Decisions etc., as well as the schedules of commitments undertaken by each Member to bind the existing degree of openness or remove existing restrictions.

Of importance to developing countries is the fact that virtually all Member have made commitments on the movement of natural persons, even if these are circumscribed by the requirement of intra-corporate transferee status. In addition, commitments made by developed countries generally cover the cross-border supply of labour-intensive services such as computer-related services, professional and construction services. Further, most developing countries have committed themselves to bind or liberalise tourism and travel service, including, for example, the liberalisation of foreign investment restrictions for hotel and resort operators. These commitments are likely to improve the supply capacity of this key sector, which provides the major source of foreign exchange earnings in a number of island developing countries and least-developed countries. In addition, a number of developing countries have taken the opportunity the GATS provides to schedule commitments, thereby binding their own domestic reform process. Improvements in the quality of service that will result from liberalisation and increased competition will contribute to improved efficiency, consumer welfare and growth in developing countries as well as all other countries.

Intellectual Property Rights

Under the WTO, the number of countries providing

intellectual property protection will increase over time. Developed countries have one year to meet their obligations, developing countries have five years and least developed countries have eleven years, with the possibility of an extension. Special transitional arrangements apply in the situation where a developing country does not presently provide patent protection in a particular chemical.

Adherence to the Paris and Berne Conventions is fairly widespread among developing countries. Many developing countries already provide minimum standards of intellectual property protection on a national treatment basis, although the scope of such protection varies significantly. Potential benefits for developing countries emerging from the Uruguay Round include a framework more conducive to domestic research efforts and to technology transfer and foreign direct investment. There will, however, be additional administrative burdens on enforcing such rights (specifically dealt with under the TRIPs Agreement), potentially higher royalty payments and adjustment costs for industries which, in the absence of domestic legislation in the area, were producing goods that would be considered as counterfeit in the future. These will also be requirements relating to patents which may well mean an increase in prices of certain goods in some developing countries. Pharmaceutical and agricultural products present examples. These increases are expected to be small, and there are provisions in the Agreement itself to minimise any adverse implications for developing countries.

Dispute Settlement

From the perspective of developing countries, it should be noted that the elements of the 1966 Decision on Dispute Settlement will continue to apply under the WTO dispute settlement procedures. Although this Decision has seldom been used, mainly because developing countries have only recently become more frequent users of the GATT dispute settlement procedures, it contains features of specific interest to developing countries, including automatic access to the "good offices" of the Director-General of the GATT/WTO to mediate and seek to find a satisfactory resolution to the dispute, and shorter time-limits in which panels must complete their deliberations.

Monitoring of Trade Policies

The TPRM provide for a Trade Policies Review Body to examine regularly the trade policies and practices of Members, every two years for the four major traders (the EU, US, Japan and Canada), every four years for the next sixteen leading traders, and every six years for the remaining traders, although longer intervals may be prescribed for least-developed countries.

The TPR process has helped countries assess their trade and economic reforms, and may have contributed to some portion of the liberalisation that has taken place under the Uruguay Round. In the future, the TPR process will help WTO Members evaluate their implementation of the Agreements, as well as provide an early warning of trends of potential concern to all participants in the trading system.

9

The Marrakesh Declaration

Ministers, representing the 124 Governments and the European Communities participating in the Uruguay Round adopted the following declaration. Ministers' salute the historic achievement represented by the conclusion of the Round, which they believe, will strengthen the world economy and lead to more trade, investment, employment and income growth throughout the world. In particular, they welcome:

- The stronger and clearer legal framework they have adopted for the conduct of international trade, including a more effective and reliable dispute settlement mechanism.
- The global reduction by 40 per cent of tariffs and wider market opening agreement on goods, and the increased predictability and security represented by a major expansion in the scope of tariff commitments, and
- The establishment of a multilateral framework of disciplines for trade in services and for the protection of trade-related intellectual property rights, as well as the reinforced multilateral trade provisions in agriculture and in textiles and clothing.

Ministers affirm that the establishment of the World Trade Organisation (WTO) ushers in a new era of global economic cooperation, reflecting the widespread desire to operate in a fairer and more open multilateral trading system for the benefit and welfare of their peoples. Ministers express their determination to resist protectionist pressures of all kinds. They believe that the trade liberalisation and strengthened rules achieved in the Uruguay Round will lead to a progressively more open world trading environment. Ministers undertake, with immediate effect and until the entry into force of the WTO, not to take any trade measures that would undermine or adversely affect the results of the Uruguay Round negotiations or their implementation.

Ministers confirm their resolution to strive for greater global coherence of policies in the fields of trade, money and finance, including cooperation between the WTO, the IMF and the World Bank for that purpose.

Ministers welcome the fact that participation in the Uruguay Round was considerably wider than in any previous multilateral trade negotiation and, in particular, that developing countries played a notably active role in it. This has marked a historic step towards a more balanced and integrated global trade partnership. Ministers note that during the period these negotiations were underway significant measures of economic reform and autonomous trade liberalisation were implemented in many developing countries and formerly centrally planned economies.

Ministers recall that the results of the negotiations embody provisions conferring differential and more favourable treatment for developing economies, including special attention to the particular situation of least-developed countries. Ministers recognize the importance of the implementation of these provisions for the least-developed countries and declare their intention to continue to assist and facilitate the expansion of their trade and investment opportunities. They agree to keep under regular review by the Ministerial Conference and the appropriate organs of the WTO the impact of the results of the Round on the least-developed countries as well as on the net-food importing developing countries, with a view to fostering positive measure to enable them to achieve their development objectives. Ministers recognize the need for strengthening the capability of the GATT and the WTO to provide increased technical assistance in their areas of competence, and in particular to substantially expand its provision to the least-developed countries.

Ministers declare that their signature of the "Final Act Embodying the Results of the Uruguay Round of Multilateral Trade Negotiations" and their adoption of associated Ministerial Decisions initiates the transition from the GATT to the WTO. They have in particular established a Preparatory Committee to lay the ground for the entry into force of the WTO Agreement and commit themselves to seek to complete all steps necessary to ratify the WTO Agreement so that it can enter into force by 1 January 1995 or as early as possible thereafter. Ministers have further more adopted a Decision on Trade and Environment.

Ministers express their sincere gratitude to His Majesty King Hassan-II of his personal contribution to the success of the Ministerial Meeting, and to his Government and the people of Morocco for their warm hospitality and the excellent organisation they have provided. The fact that this final Ministerial Meeting of the Uruguay Round has been held at Marrakesh is an additional manifestation of Morocco's commitment to an open world trading system and to its fullest integration to the global economy.

With the adoption and signature of the Final Act and the opening for acceptance of the WTO Agreement, Ministers declare the work of the Trade Negotiations Committee to be complete and the Uruguay Round formally concluded.

***

10

Winners and Losers

The WTO and the Developing Countries

The World Trade Organisation (WTO) began work on January 1, 1995. The new international body's tasks include implementing the results of the Uruguay Round, which reach far beyond the old General Agreement of Tariffs and Trade (GATT). Besides the traditional GATT remit of overseeing trade in goods, the results of the eighth round of GATT talks encompass among other things rules on trade in services, protecting intellectual property, and wider institutional competences in settling trade disputes. Furthermore, GATT's old no-go areas such as trade in agro-products, textiles and clothing, were integrated in its body of rules.

The role and participation of developing countries underwent considerable changes during the course of the new Uruguay Round. Before the talks began, many governments of the south took a highly critical stance on the taking up of the negotiations, and above all on the widening of their brief. Leading critics among the developing countries, such as Brazil and India, called for the effective implementation of the results of the Tokyo Round (1973-79) before beginning new talks. This thumbs-down gave a glimpse once again of the unity of developing countries, which during the 1970s set the trade policy agenda and contributed to the flourishing of the UN Conference on Trade and Development (UNCTAD). But their increasing differences in economic interests were soon reflected in disparate negotiating positions during the GATT talks. In some sectors such as agricultural trade, the developing countries no longer had any common interests whatsoever. Nevertheless, both during and after the round there were various attempts to assess the possible impacts of trade liberalisation on the developing countries as a whole. The World Bank and the OECD's Development Assistance Committee tried very early in the negotiations to make the possible results palatable for the developing countries with encouraging projections. The developing countries' high rate of accession to the WTO reflects the growing importance of the world trade order for them. And many of them are meanwhile pushing ahead with liberalisation of their own economies, partly of their own accord and partly in the context of structural adjustment programmes. But they often evaluate the results of the Uruguay Round quite differently. The following is aimed at summarising briefly the possible political and economic impacts of the developing countries, which have been the subject of debate so far.

Stricter Rules on World Trade

The Uruguay Round led to a widening and strengthening of the body of rules on world trade. Its widening covered the inclusion of the above mentioned new sectors and the old areas of exception. Its strengthening relates to the drawing up of stricter rules for fixing standards to counter the growing use of non-tariff obstacles to trade, and to the new procedure for settling disputes. While under the old rules all treaty states had to approve the ruling of an arbitration procedure—including the "loser" country—to make it valid, an arbitration now takes effect directly. Only its unanimous rejection by the treaty signatories can make it null and void.

NGOs in the North and the South in particular interpret both the widening and strengthening critically. In their view, the changes give the WTO too much power. They fear that national political decisions in future could be assessed and attacked as possible trade obstacles. They say this reduces the already limited possibilities of nation states to determine important policy fields, such as the environment and social or regional policy.

Strong and Weak Members

However, to what extent these legal remedies can actually be resorted to in the everyday life of global trade policy remains to be seen in the near future. As early as during US ratification of the Uruguay Round, the Clinton Administration commented that if USA were to be censured three times by a GATT dispute process it would reserve the right to leave the organisation again. Since weaker trade partners lack the possibility to take pain-inflicting countermeasures, the different trade policy weights of the WTO members will also count in future practice.

The estimates of individual groups of developing countries on possible economic profits stemming from Uruguay Round differ greatly. Projections of potential trade profits were downright euphoric even before the end of the negotiations.

The general reduction of custom duties on industrial goods—put about 37 per cent—will impact on the developing countries as a whole because the previous preferential tariffs will become relatively less important. There will be few changes for countries that have so far hardly taken advantage of preferences. But the cutback will impact in particular on African countries, which have the most extensive preferences, as well as on the ASEAN group, which were especially high users of the Generalised System of Preferences. A loss of 1.5 per cent is projected for Sub-Saharan Africa and the ACP states, and 1.9 per cent for LDC's. According to Overseas Development Institute (ODI) estimates, the figures for individual countries could be much worse. Ethiopia, Malawi, Mozambique and Guayana are likely to lose between 4.6 per cent and 5.9 per cent of their export earings.

Agricultural Markets Remain Distorted

In the agricultural sector, the net food importers among the developing countries will be losers because they will have to pay moderately higher prices for their imports. The forecasts of losses, however, are not so high since no far-reaching liberalisation can be achieved in the agro-sector. The two main adversaries in Uruguay Round's dispute over agriculture, the USA and the EU, were able in the Blair House Agreement to reach an accord on only a very limited reduction of their high support payments to their farmers. Even cutbacks in export subsidies were pegged at about only 21 per cent in volume and about 36 per cent in value. That is why export subsidies will continue to exert pressure on world market prices. At the same time, the slight reduction will mean the net agricultural produce exporters among the developing countries will derive only marginal profit from the liberalisation.

On the positive side, the most important sector of projected profits for developing countries is textiles and clothing. The accord on these goods foresees the previous Multifibre Agreement (MFA) expiring within 10 years and textiles and clothing coming step-by-step under GATT rules. But is remains to be seen if that target can be achieved in that period, and how often in future the industrial countries will invoke the protective clause covering this sector to safeguard their own industries.

Weak States will Lose

Taking an overall look at the results of the Uruguay Round, it can be noted that those developing countries, which are strong in exports of industrial goods and have so far hardly used the Generalised System of Preference, will profit economically. The losers will be countries, which will suffer from the erosion of the importance of preferences. Totting up, negative impacts of more than US $2 billion are forecast for Africa. Various sides—NGOs as well as some governments—are therefore now calling for compensation payments for net losers.

The developing countries lost unity came to life again towards the end of the Uruguay Round when new subjects for world trade order were put on the agenda. Some governments and NGOs are increasingly addressing the ecological and social impacts of the liberalisation of world trade. They are above all highly vocal in expressing fears that the globalisation of the world economy will be accompanied by a loss of national sovereignty over political measures in sectors such as the environment and social and regional policy. And that linked with an increasingly competitive situation in an ever more open world market. This will in the long-term have negative impacts on a country's ability to assert justified measures to protect its interests. The governments of most developing countries have clearly rejected these new proposals for discussion. They fear this bid could make the industrial nations' hopes for economic protectionism reappear.

New Role for WTO

There is no simple answer to these new agendas. Indeed, it is questionable if the WTO is a suitable forum to negotiate on them in detail. However, so long as a relatively effective governing body on world trade relations has no counterpart in comparably effective instruments to deal with the social and ecological impacts of globalisation, there will probably be repeated attempts to assign new competences to the WTO. Even when it would make more sense not to leave multilateral rules on environmental protection or securing human rights to a trade organisation. That nothing should block the objectives of sustainable development or safeguarding human rights, which go beyond trade policy, must thereby be beyond doubt.

❊ ❊ ❊

11

Developing Countries and the WTO Agricultural Negotiations

Developing countries as a group have much to gain from continued progress toward a transparent, rule based trading system in agriculture. The researchers say the negotiations should eliminate export subsidies, impose stricter disciplines on export taxes, cut tariffs, and ensure that food aid continues to be available to poor countries in grant form and delivered so as not to displace domestic production in the countries receiving it. Badly managed food aid, or cheap food imports due to export subsidies, may just reinforce the bias of economic policies against the rural sector. With its negative impact on poor agricultural producers, they say. International research organisations (such as IFPRI, among other institutions) may provide support to developing countries through programmes of collaborative research, technical assistance, and capacity strengthening.

Starting with the first round of trade negotiations under the General Agreement on Tariffs and Trade (GATT) after World War II, there has been a relatively steady trend of increasing multilateral trade liberalisation. The successive rounds of negotiations recognised the greater needs of developing countries, especially since the Tokyo Round. Yet the participation of developing countries was limited. Since many developing countries were not members of GATT, the major forum for airing their views was provided by the United Nations Conference on Trade and Development. The views of developing countries had some impact on the Lome agreements and on aid flows, but had limited influence on negotiations concerning trading rules, which were discussed within the framework of the GATT, where OECD (Organisation for Economic Cooperation and Development) countries set the agenda.

In the Uruguay Round, which began in 1986 and concluded in 1993, developing countries played a larger role in the negotiations compared to previous rounds. In particular, agricultural net exporters organised the Cairns Group (which in addition to Australia, New Zealand, and Canada, included several large developing countries such as Argentina, Brazil, Indonesia, and the Philippines) to pursue their interests. Furthermore, during and after the conclusion of the Uruguay Round, the formal accession of developing countries to the GATT and now the World Trade Organisation (WTO) has continued apace. Of the 134 members of the WTO in February 1999, some 70 per cent were developing countries. The United Nations classified 48 countries as least-developed (LLDCs). Within that group, 29 are members of the WTO, six are in the process of accession, and three are observers. Also, 18 countries have been identified as net-food-importing developing countries (NFIDCs).

Some Definitions

The LLDCs are identified by the United Nations General Assembly based on several criteria—income per capita, augmented physical quality of life index, and an index of economic diversification. As a group, they have a population of about 590 million people, with an income per capita about 4 per cent that of the world average (1996). Agricultural production per capita in LLDCs has been declining since the 1970s although the same indicator for all developing countries (mainly under the influence of China) has gone up by nearly 40 per cent in the same period. LLDCs represent a small fraction of world trade (less than 1 per cent for total and about 2 per cent for agricultural trade). They had a positive, although declining net agricultural trade balance until the mid 1980s, when it turned negative. Almost 20 per cent of their total imports are food items.

The 18 net-food-importing developing countries have been selected through a process within the WTO. They have a population of some 380 million people and an income per capita nearly five times that of the LLDC average, but still much lower than the world average. NFIDCs are a diverse group: four are upper-middle income countries; eight are lower-middle income; and six are lower income. Four of them had net food exports on average during 1995-97, but because they imported cereals they are included in the group. NFIDCs' per capita food production as share of both world and developing country averages has risen, although from very low levels.

Although the categories of "developed" and "developing" countries have important legal consequences under WTO rules, there are no formal definitions of either category. The process works through self-identification and negotiation with other member countries of the WTO.

Completing the Unfinished Agenda

In general, developing countries operate under what has been called "special and differential treatment". They face lower disciplines and enjoy longer time frames for implementing reforms. In the case of LLDCs, they are totally exempted from WTO commitments, and it has been agreed that developing and least-developed countries should receive special consideration for market access and technical and financial support. Also, during the Uruguay Round, concerns that liberalisation of agricultural policies and trade could adversely affect the food imports of LLDCs and NFIDCs led participants to include several measures dealing with food security issues in the "green box" of permitted domestic support—for instance, the formation of public stockholding and the provision of foodstuffs at subsidised prices. There was a ministerial decision in Marrakesh in April 1994 to deal with possible negative effects of agricultural trade reforms on the food security of LLDCs and NFIDCs. The decision was reemphasised at the 1996 ministerial meeting of the WTO in Singapore.

Export and Domestic Subsidies: While many developing countries have significantly reduced distorting domestic agricultural policies, the possible benefits that these countries and the world can enjoy are thwarted by the subsidies of developed countries. The Uruguay Round was a first step in imposing discipline on the unfair competition arising from subsidised agricultural exports, which hurts poor agricultural producers in developing countries irrespective of their net agricultural trade position. In the next negotiations, that first step should be completed with the elimination of export subsidies. Net-food-importing developing countries should also be interested in stricter disciplines on export taxes and controls that exacerbate price fluctuations in world markets.

Under the Uruguay Round agreement, there is still a lot of scope for the developed countries to use domestic subsidies, in addition to the use of export subsidies; to help their farmers. The developing countries should seek further disciplines in this regard, including, among other things, the elimination of exemptions under the "blue box" (which allows farmers to receive some forms of direct payments that are considered to be trade distorting). Least-developed and developing countries, however, will still be allowed "special and differential treatment" on these issues.

Market Access: If the developing countries are to succeed in diversifying their agricultural sectors, they need expanded access to markets in developed countries. This includes increasing the volume of imports allowed under the current regime of tariff-rate quotas (TRQs, which replaced the previous system of rigid quotas with a combination of a quantitative quota and a high tariff for the eventual out-of-quota imports); making the administration of the TRQs more transparent and equitable; seeking further reductions in tariffs, particularly those still high in some key products; and completing the process of tariffication in the cases where exemptions were granted. Also, eliminating, or at least reducing, tariffs escalation in non-agricultural products is important for developing countries: this practice undermines the possibilities of expanding production and exports of processed goods that use agricultural inputs, exploiting "forward linkages" in the value-added chain.

What the Most Vulnerable Need

The special situation and concerns of least-developed countries and net-food-importing countries were recognised in a ministerial decision agreed upon at the completion of the Uruguay Round in 1993. These concerns include the preservation of adequate levels of food aid, the provision of technical assistance and financial support to develop the agricultural sector in those countries, and the continuation and expansion of financial facilities to help with structural adjustment and short-term difficulties in financing food imports. It is important to make food aid available in grant form, to target it to poor countries and social groups, and to deliver it in ways that do not displace domestic production in the countries receiving it. Badly managed food aid, or cheap food imports due to export subsidies, may just reinforce the bias of economic policies against the rural sector, with its negative impact on poor agricultural producers.

Volatility in agricultural prices must be monitored carefully. While expansion of world agricultural trade should limit overall fluctuations by spreading supply and demand shocks over larger areas, the decline in world public stocks as a percentage of consumption works in the opposite direction. Improving early warning of potential food shortages, lowering costs for food transportation and storage, and providing better targeted food aid programmes and financial facilities for emergencies are also issues that need to be addressed by countries participating in the coming round of negotiations.

The impact of changes in trade and agricultural policy on poorer consumers and producers in developing countries is a matter of debate. Some have argued that trade liberalisation may hurt both groups. Others have answered that greater productivity and growth coming from better trade and sectoral policies should help generate employment and income, given a setting of adequate overall economic policies and properly functioning markets and social institutions.

Small producers will also be helped by the disciplines that the URAA is bringing to subsidised and dumped exports, while it allows the implementation of a variety of programmes aimed at poor producers or consumers, including stocks for food security purposes and domestic food aid for populations in need. The issue here is the adequate design and funding of domestic policies to achieve the intended objectives of agricultural growth and poverty alleviation, which most certainly will not be helped by trade-distorting interventions either in developed or developing countries.

In general, low-income developing countries and LLDCs should emphasise to the international community the importance of creating and expanding a supportive international trade and financial environment and of implementing an integrated framework for economic and social development, with agricultural and trade polices being an integral part of the strategy. Appropriate measures would include—in addition to the agricultural trade issues suggested here—the continuation and enhancement of the reduction of the external debt of Heavily Indebted Poor Countries (The HIPC initiative) and the further liberalisation of trade in textiles.

But improved international conditions should go hand-in-hand with a better domestic framework in developing and least-developed countries, including stable macro-economic policies, open and effective markets, good governance, the rule of law, a vibrant civil society, and programmes and investments that expand opportunities for all, with special consideration for poor and disadvantaged groups.

Bringing Developing Countries into the Process

Developing countries, as small players in the global arena, should be interested and active participants in the design and implementation of international rules that limit the ability of larger countries to resort to unilateral action. Also, domestic legal and institutional frameworks in developing countries may be strengthened by the implementation of internationally negotiated rules that limit the scope for rent seeking and arbitrary projectionist measures. The developing countries as a group have much to gain from continued progress toward a transparent, rule-based, trading system in agriculture.

What are the requirements and skills for the developing countries to become effective members in the next WTO round? Any negotiation requires careful consideration of the legal, economic, and political dimensions that define the substance and possible evolution of the negotiations, as well as the diplomatic and negotiating techniques that may help in the attainment of the expected outcomes. Questions that need to be addressed include:

- What are the economic and social consequences of different WTO scenarios (quantitative estimation of impacts)? Knowing the impacts of alternative scenarios is crucial if developing countries are to represent their interests in the negotiation process;
- What are the legal issues being discussed (definition of obligations, exemptions, time frame, and so on)? Detailed knowledge of international trade law is crucial if developing countries are not to be "shortchanged." The devil is in the details;
- Looking at the political process, who are the main actors and their interests and what type of alliances may drive the negotiations? Negotiators must understand the political economy of their own country and of other countries in the WTO if they are to negotiate effectively;

- With these elements, an adequate diplomatic and negotiating strategy must be defined and implemented.

Developing countries that have carefully considered all four components will be better prepared to participate effectively in the coming negotiations. Of course, limited financial and human resources act as an important constraint. However, developing countries may overcome some of the problems through collective action, for instance considering the creation of alliances with respect to their main export and import commodities and the markets they approach for their exports. An example is the Cairns Group. This approach could reduce the fixed costs of negotiations. Spreading them over groups of countries, allow a better use of scarce technical expertise, and improve the bargaining position of developing countries. It could also be in the interest of the OECD countries to deal with negotiating blocs, which represent a smaller number of negotiating positions, rather than with numerous separate countries. The negotiations would be much more efficient and balanced.

❋❋❋

12

The Future of Agricultural Trade

In the Uruguay Round, countries recognised that the long term solution for agriculture did not lie in administered prices, trade restrictions, supply controls and export subsidies but rather in open, non-distorted markets. It is the time to take bold steps toward bringing agricultural trade into the 21st century by accelerating agricultural trade reform.

There are four key areas for accelerating reforms: eliminating export subsidies; increasing market access through substantial tariff cuts and expansion of tariff rate quotas; cutting further trade-distorting domestic subsidies; and ensuring technical standards are based on sound science.

The world's farmers and ranchers are facing two difficult challenges at the dawn of the 21st century. First, they are being asked to provide more products at lower cost, higher quality, greater variety, and in a safer manner than ever demanded before. Second, they are being asked to produce this abundance on a shrinking natural resources base that is often subject to government regulations. Meeting these global challenges will require unleashing the production potential of world agriculture while practising proper environmental stewardship. The ingenuity and hardwork we usually associate with farmers will be essential to meet these challenges, but they will not be sufficient unless we further reform agricultural trade to create an environment that rewards risk and investment and encourages efficiencies.

Today's Agricultural Challenges

Farmers are responsible for feeding a rapidly growing world population. And despite progress over the years, too many people still are not getting enough food. Many countries including the United States, are working vigorously to promote technological innovations to meet the need for food and fiber in the coming years. However, as important as this work is, it is only part of the solution. These technologies and the hard work of the world's farmers need a trading environment that encourages investment and efficient production, and generates economic growth to finance production and consumption needs long-term trends in agriculture pose serious challenges for all farmers. The same technological advances that increase yields may result in lower prices. Increasing social concerns about effect of agricultural production on the environment and living conditions result in new restrictions on farm activities. As urban dwellers and industry stake competing claims for land, water and energy, many producers find their ability to farm made ever more difficult.

Two approaches to organising the agricultural economy present a stark contrast in dealing with these challenges. One model, popular in Europe and Asia, is to retain an inward-looking agricultural system focused on supply control and government regulation geared to keeping farm prices high and, since guaranteed high prices are a drain on the treasury, to controlling production. Under this approach, bureaucrats try to assess the optimal level of national production—not so little that imports are needed and not so much that excess production; must be bought at high prices and then dumped on world markets. This "command-and-control" structure stifles farmer efficiency and ingenuity and distorts world markets, especially as subsidised surpluses are regularly exported; and it does not address the challenge to farmers to produce food for the next century. It also ignores the interest of domestic consumers (who have to pay high internal prices) and producers in other countries (who have to compete with subsidised products). Of biggest concern is that the anti-market policies of this approach hamstring the agriculture sector from pursuing the technological advances needed to meet its future challenges.

Another approach is to place agriculture on a more market-oriented basis, particularly by removing trade barriers and reducing trade-distorting policies. Greater market orientation was the principle that actions agreed to in the last set of multilateral trade negotiations. In the Uruguay Round, countries recognised that the long-term solution for agriculture did not lie in administered prices, trade restrictions, supply controls, and export subsidies but rather in open, non-distorted markets. Now is the time to take bold steps toward bringing agricultural trade into the 21st century by accelerating agricultural trade reform.

The Gains from Trade

The benefit from free and fair trading of agricultural products have immediate effects on people. Eliminating trade barriers and reducing unfair competition will help ensure that farmers have incentives to produce and consumers have access to the products they desire. Liberalising agricultural trade will contribute to better resource allocation by farmers, which has conservation benefits, rewards low-cost producers, encourages efficiencies, and removes the drag on economic growth.

Opening trading opportunities also increases the food security of food-importing countries by giving supplier countries the confidence required to put more land into production and to create marketing relationships. Trade provides consumers with year-round access to a greater variety of less expensive products, while rewarding producers who are able to find and meet specific consumer demands for high-value products. In a broader context, by allowing imports that are more efficiently produced elsewhere, trade encourages specialisation in efficient agricultural and non-agricultural production.

More dramatically, trade literally saves lives. Without the international flow of food products from areas with abundant production to areas where food is scarce, many people in the world would be eating less or not at all. Trade has dynamic effects, as well, that push long-term productivity growth. For example, access to customers in overseas markets creates an incentive for technological innovation, resulting in exciting developments in improved seed varieties and production techniques. International markets also expand market outlets, raising prices and giving producers increased confidence to produce more than required merely for national needs, allowing productive farmers to not only feed their neighbours but literally feed the world.

Equally important, trade in agricultural products is becoming increasingly critical to farm and ranch incomes. Increased productivity and often times flat domestic demand increases the importance of reliable international markets. Foreign markets are not just a dumping ground for surplus products; overseas consumers value choice and quality, particularly when producers in their own country cannot meet their demands or when they are charged inflated prices. Consequently foreign and value-added agricultural producers, raising farm-gate prices and helping support the range of agriculture-related industries.

Political reality also encourages a focus on international markets; policies based on high government guaranteed prices are ultimately politically untenable because they are hugely expensive, unresponsive to the needs of customers and producers, insensitive to environmental and agronomic realities, and a shameful waste of economic assets. Rather than farming government programmes, our producers are looking for customers around the world.

While agricultural trade benefits consumers and producers alike, it is an area in which progressive reform is ardently opposed by entrenched domestic interests. Producers in some countries, cosseted by high guaranteed prices and protective tariffs, oppose any move toward greater market orientation. Intervention in the agricultural economy—measured by the Organisation for Economic Cooperation and Development by summing price supports, direct payments, and other support as a per cent of total agricultural production—has actually increased in some countries from the levels at the beginning of the Uruguay Round. In the last set of multilateral trade negotiations, countries began the process of dismantling protection and delinking farm support from production decisions. Consequently, reforms have been undertaken by some countries.

The WTO Opportunity

The major objective in the upcoming farm talks is to accelerate the reform process initiated in the Uruguay Round. That means further substantial negotiations on tariffs, subsidies, and other trade-distorting measures so that the level and other trade-distorting measures so that the level and direction of trade are determined by market forces, not government intervention. Four key areas are outlined below:

(i) ***Export Competition:*** Export subsidies are the most distorting trade tool because the level and direction of trade is directly determined by government subsidies. Today, the European Union (EU) is the only substantial export subsidizer—nearly all other countries agreed not to use, or have only limited resource to use, export subsidies in the last round of negotiations. EU farmers, responding to domestic prices frequently twice the world price, produce more products than can be consumed in Europe, but at such high prices that they can be sold abroad only with generous subsidies. These subsidies push other competitive supplies out of the market (which is expensive and unfair) and discourage production in countries that have a comparative advantage in agricultural production (which is wasteful and is threatening both to the environment and to future farm production needs).

In the Uruguay Round negotiations, countries acknowledged the corrosive nature of subsidies and agreed to cap and reduce their use. The upcoming negotiations should eliminate them to ensure that countries do not resort to other policy tools that allow government spending to determine winners in the marketplace. Specifically, WTO members should look closely at curbing distorting state trading agricultural export monopolies that can disguise subsidies and exert distorting market power, along with other policies used to dispose of surplus commodities on a non-market basis.

(ii) Market Access: Measure applied at the border to stop trade currently are the principal barrier to a freer and more open trading environment for agriculture. Market access barriers deny efficient producers the chance to compete in other markets and limit the variety and quality of products available to consumers. Opening markets and maximising trade opportunities are fundamental principles of WTO, and we still have a long way to go in agriculture to open markets to competition.

The Uruguay Round Agreement set agricultural trade on a more predictable basis by requiring that all non-tariff measures, such as quotas and import bans be converted to simple tariffs. While this was a necessary first step to removing trade barriers, many of the tariffs are still prohibitively high. For example, while the average tariff assessed by the United States on agricultural products is less than 5 per cent (and nearly zero for industrial products), the average agriculture tariff rate quota (TRQ). Where only specific quantities of imports receive low duties. Many other commodities also; are subject to high tariffs.

As we start the next century, higher tariffs should not stop the flow of imported agricultural products. Where TRQs remain as a transitional step before we achieve more open trade, we expect more specific disciplines on the way in which they are administered. Similarly, we need to take a hard look at agricultural state trading monopoly. Importers; use of these state traders may have been justifiable when more restrictions allowed on farm trade, but in the tariff-only regime it is hard to see why a government needs to insert itself between an exports and an end-user.

(iii)Domestic Subsidies: Domestic subsidy programmes are often the root cause of other-distorting polices. Subsidy policies that increase domestic prices above world price levels can be maintained only if price-competitive imports are restricted. Additionally, overproduction generated by high domestic prices can be sold on world markets only with export subsidies that bring the price down to the world price. While reining in distortive domestic subsidy programmes has value in its own right for rationalising agricultural production, the WTO negotiations will focus on their trade-distorting elements.

In the Uruguay Round negotiations, countries agreed to distinguish trade-distorting subsidies (generally those linked to the production of a specific crop or related to price supports) from non-trade distorting subsidies (such as research and development, training and environmental production). The trade-distorting subsidies were capped, and the process of reducing allowable levels of subsidies began. This distinction is a good one: the nasty sort of subsidy that distorts markets and straitjackets producers should be cut, while programmes that will increase a country's ability to produce agricultural products in the next century without distorting production incentives should not be reduced.

(iv) Standards: As WTO members make progress on cutting tariffs and subsidies, the temptation increase to disguise trade barriers as health and safety measures or other innocuous-sounding "technical standards". Moreover, when regulations purportedly designed to protect heath are instead vehicles for domestic protectionism, the credibility

> of the entire safety apparatus of a country is put up for questioning. When good science is replaced by politics, the basis for sound health policy is undermined. Therefore, increasing government accountability by putting the emphasis on sound science for health standards should discipline disguised barriers to trade and strengthen health policy.

In the Uruguay Round, countries agreed to a set of sound principles: each has the right to maintain health and safety measures, but these must be based on sound science, backed by scientific evidence and an assessment of the risk, and be no more trade-restrictive than required to meet health goals. In practice, countries have found that these principles work well—bogus measures adopted without scientific basis have been successfully challenged in the WTO without sacrificing health concerns. Creating a supportive environment for the propagation of yield-enhancing biotech products also is critical for meeting the needs of the coming century.

Agriculture is Different

Agriculture occupies a special place in the national economies of most countries around the world. Farmers are responsible for feeding and clothing people. Farming also holds a powerful claim on our national cultures that calls for the preservation of rural lifestyles and values. Farm production is subject to the cruel vagaries of weather and the relentless decline in prices and increases in costs. Some people point to these factors as justifying a different treatment for agriculture in the international economy, including justifying trade-distorting agricultural policies. This is wrong-headed; societies can support farms and preserve rural communities in ways that foster choice, protect natural resources, and expand trade.

Farm production in the next century cannot afford to be trapped in a static system in which prices are determined by government mandate, production decisions are controlled by central planners, and farmers are forced to produce only for local consumers. This myopic system cannot be sustained in any important agriculture producing society. Moreover, this type of system will not meet the needs of the coming century, when we will face unprecedented consumer demand and natural resource constraints.

Instead, I look forward to dynamic world of agricultural trade in which producers, exporters and retailers apply the creativity of the human mind to the natural bounty of the earth. In this "new" world, we will produce a greater amount and variety of food than ever before, feed the coming billions, sustain our environment, and unlock economic resources otherwise stifled by moribund protectionism, ultimately raising living standards around the world.

13

ASEAN—Regional Trade and Sustainability

Many Small and Medium Enterprises (SMEs) see globalisation as more of a threat than an oppurtunity. They are worried that the competitive advantages for transnational companies will make it harder, even impossible for them to gain market access. Even though such fears are not groundless, there are certainly international markets which are accessible for SMEs and where the characteristic features of SMEs are a distinct advantage. The markets in question are those across the border in neighbouring countries.

Indeed, trade between neighbours accounts for a much bigger portion of international trade than most people think. Throughout history, trade has always flourished where borders were drawn between countries because it is easier to do business with a neighbour than with an anonymous partner in some far-off land. Even in the European Union, for example, the lion's share of international business is transacted between trading partners no more than 100 kilometers apart in neighbouring countries a state of affairs which has helped promote SMEs running cross-border operations on a regional level.

Economists have long been reluctant to focus on regional trade agreements. But the more business and even governments discover their importance, the more economic theory has to take them into account. Today, we know that promoting regional trade secures profit margins which far outstrip any that can be hoped for on the global stage. What's more, those profits are enjoyed by large, medium and small-scale companies.

Sustainable Development

Sustainable development is now acknowledged throughout the world as a model principle for future economic activity. Sustainability encompasses careful management of the environment, consideration for local traditions and respect for the needs of the poor. It is an easy concept to define, especially in the context of political programmes and executive orders.

Sustainable development also embraces the need to adapt ideal-case objectives to specific-local conditions. Here, care for the environment and poverty reduction action are two sides of the same coin-sustainable success is possible only where working principles are firmly rooted in local environmental and social conditions. However reasonable this sounds, it is actually a source of tension, upset and provocation between sustainable development and international economic policy in general and structural adjustment and trade liberalisation in particular. In the latter instance especially, attempts are commonly made to apply principles which are not attuned to local conditions. One of the main criticisms of the IMF's response to the Asian crisis, for example, is that it sought to apply a standard solution to a totally new situation without taking account of special local conditions.

ASEAN—The Asean Perspective

Strengthening economic relations and leberalising trade between regional partners with a view to securing closer cooperation is known as "integration". Here, countries formulate and coordinate jointly defined action to ensure that environmentally relevant, social and cultural developments in each individual country are respected and the needs and requirements and neighbours remain in sharp focus.

Asia is a region which in recent years has increasingly set its sights on economic integration. The Association of South East Asian nations, ASEAN, has fully embraced the cause of introducing and developing a regional economic policy. Aside from working to wards more regional cooperation, its members have also agreed to strengthen and embark on cooperative projects in the commodity, food and energy sectors. With the establishment of the free trade zone AFTA (ASEAN free trade area), a counterweight was created to the regional economic areas of the west.

The question today is whether ASEAN will succeed and whether that, in turn, will promote the political integration of the region. The organisation's continued existence depends mainly on foreign policy interests and political stability in the region. Pessimists see at least three obstacles to swift and extensive economic integration: lack of progress by ASEAN countries towards the internal stability needed for long-term regional ties, diversity of political cultures and interests, and weak leadership within ASEAN.

Indeed, the political legacies, cultures and visions of the association's members are fundamentally different. ASEAN is in an unstable, unpredictable political environment. South East Asia is the major political theatre in the war against terrorism. Indonesia is experiencing a turbulent transition to democracy. Serious differences and disputes among ASEAN members have increased. And there is no sign of the strong leadership that could smooth out the troubles within the association. Against this backdrop, it is not surprising that there has been neither political nor organisational progress towards pan ASEAN structures which could promote economic integration.

❋ ❋ ❋

14

The World Bank Needs Innovative Theory

The World Bank's macroeconomic assumptions disregard many issues relevant to development. These include, for instance, population growth and income distribution. Endogenous growth models are better suited to analyse complex interactions than the conventional tools of neoclassic and post-Keynesian economics.

The World Bank is officially committed to sustainable development. Yet its own policy does not adhere to this principle. Structural adjustment programmes and poverty reduction strategies still conflict with social and ecological goals. One reason for the poor sustainability record is the World Bank's outdated theoretical approach based on neoclassic and post-Keynesian ideas.

Both are incompatible with sustainability. Neoclassic understanding of sustainability rests on the belief that technological progress automatically leads to a more efficient use of resources and, accordingly, to less ecological degradation.

For several reasons, post-Keynesian models are similarly incompatible with the principle of sustainability. First of all, they produce analyses for the short-term. Typically, merely two periods are considered, which is inadequate for designing a growth process in general and even more so for a sustainable path to development. Moreover, these models also disregard distribution because they only take aggregated quantities into account.

World Bank economists, however, still work with country-specific variants of the post-Keynesian Revised Minimum Standard Model, although it is academically outdated and cannot deal with the complexity of development processes. The model's merits are that it is easy to understand and apply. In addition, little information on the behaviour of the economic actors is required. The World Bank determines the volume of its loans on the basis of such calculations. In addition to the transfer of these sums, the bank believes that measures to promote growth are necessary. These are expected to be in line with the Washington Consensus approach of privatisation, deregulation and liberalisation.

The structural and stabilisation measures that the World Bank economists implement are thus based on theoretical models which are incompatible with the principle of sustainability and which they, at most, supplement with cushioning elements. The obvious alternative would be to apply more recent approaches of endogenous growth theory. After all, economic growth is a precondition for sustainable development. Endogenous growth models are very diverse, so one cannot speak of an integrated and comprehensive theory. However, all endogenous models share the attempt to explain growth without recourse to exogenous factors. While the basic model of endogenous growth theory was developed for industrialised nations, it can be adapted to situations typical of developing countries. This gives an idea of the complex interrelatedness of economic phenomena.

Complex Interactions

These manifold links clearly serve to illustrate the shortcomings of the World Bank. For example, the IMF and the World Bank call for the immediate opening of national economies to world trade. By contrast, endogenous growth models suggest assessing free trade's benefits for developing countries more diligently. Trade liberalisation only presents an opportunity to increase long-term growth rates in developing countries when pursued in a differentiated way respecting specific needs of countries and sectors. Otherwise, there is a risk of economies specializing solely on low-technology goods, which, in turn, means forsaking long-term innovation.

Complementary measures are necessary if developing countries are to take advantage of liberalisation. Education, enhancement of communications and transport infrastructure and special mechanisms for the transfer of knowledge from advanced to developing countries (such as on-the-job-training, imitation of existing technologies and foreign direct investment) are important determinants for economic development. The level of education in a developing country is particularly significant. If a national economy has too little human capital, opening the markets mostly results in minor or even negative growth effects. Empirical studies support these statements.

Population growth is a serious obstacle to development. In may poor regions, it puts the already overburdened education and health systems under additional stress. Traditional economics theory, however, ignores the significance of fertility. Endogenous growth models can take family planning into account and link birth rates to social security systems as well as to environmental aspects. Doing so leads to developmental insights. For instance, short-term social cushioning measures, such as those implemented frequently by the World Bank and its partners to reduce the negative impacts of programme-tied loans, do not suffice for a positive development process. By contrast, long-term social security measures (such as introducing a pension scheme) contribute to reducing fertility.

Poverty Stalls Growth

Incomes in developing countries are mostly distributed very unevenly. The World Bank, so far, does not view this as an important obstacle to development. At any rate, the widespread thesis that, in the wake of economic development, inequality first increases and then decreases by itself has empirically been shown to be wrong. Endogenous growth models under pin this finding in theoretical terms. Unequal income distribution results in too little investment in training, the consequences of which impede growth.

Endogenous models are also useful from an ecological viewpoint. According to neoclassic environmental and resources theory, external effects of noxious emissions and over-exploitation of resources must be internalised in order to ensure long-term economic growth. Instruments in tune with the market, such as taxes or certificates, are better suited to do so than strict governmental regulation. Even these findings are not yet paid enough attention in the Country Assistance Strategies in which the World Bank lays down short to medium-term development strategies.

Endogenous growth theory contributes to analyzing the complex interactions of sustainable development. Even if most of the recommendations are well established in the critique of developmental practice, formal theoretical analyses help to avoid the arbitrariness of policy statements. Future research must show how to develop a user-friendly, comprehensive. Building on a profound analysis of development determinants, it will be possible to draft country specific development strategies in line with sustainability principles. These should be reflected in the conditionalities of programme-tied loans. To ensure consistent implementation of sustainable development policy, the World Bank must update its theoretical models. Endogenous growth theory provides a starting point.

***

15

Taking a Lead in the Fight Against Poverty?

World Bank and IMF Speed Implementation of their New Strategy

A change in development policy strategy in the poorest countries is at present being prepared with incredible speed. The IMF-style structural adjustment programmes that have been criticised for many years are being scrapped. The countries are now to take their own decisions on their paths to development. Their governments will no longer formulate poverty reduction programmes top-down, but in an intensive and long-term dialogue with societal groups and organisations. Governments and institutions of the North commit themselves to supporting these processes, such as by debt relief on an unprecedented scale. Dream or reality?

New Strategy Paper

Behind this euphoria lines a new abbreviation, PRSP, standing for Poverty Reduction Strategy Paper, which the IMF and World Bank invented last year. The G-7 countries in Cologne not only announced debt relief for the heavily indebted poor countries (HIPCs) but also demanded that it must serve above all for poverty reduction. The PRSP concept was then presented at the annual conference of the two Bretton Woods organisations.

The most important principles of the new "super weapon" in the fight against poverty are:

- PRSPs are papers, which describe the medium-term development paths of the poorest countries of the

South, particularly their strategies to combat poverty, and by this means enlist international support. A PRSP is not only the prerequisite for granting debt forgiveness in the context of the HIPC initiative. It is also necessary for all new IMF and World Bank loans to the so-called IDA countries, the some 70 poorest countries that receive concessional loans from the World Bank's International Development Agency (IDA). According to the World Bank, PRSPs should also be required for all future pledges of bilateral development assistance.

- Not only social sector programmes, but also the economic and financial policies of the developing countries are in future to be aimed at fighting poverty. Previously, the IMF always pronounced that a growth-oriented national economy and a far-reaching integration in the world market would have a trickle-down effect and also benefit the poor. Now the poor are to be asked what policies can help materially to improve their situation.
- PRSPs are to be developed on the basis of self-responsible country ownership. Accordingly, development and structural adjustment strategies are no longer to be developed by the Washington finance institutions, but the countries themselves.
- The heading "country ownership" is to underline that not only governments are called upon, PRSPs should come into being in a participatory process. That means involvement of trade unions, NGOs cooperatives, associations, grassroots groups, political parties and parliaments. A country's PRSP should be developed in a societal debate, a dialogue between governments on one side and parliamentary, private sector and civil society on the other.

Rhetoric or Reality?

Are PRSPs the expression of a change of paradigm? In

brief, if all what the papers contain is implemented in a consistent and wide-ranging, way, the chances of achieving it are good but there are a number of open questions. The answers to them will have a bearing on success or failure.

Is the IMF really changing its policy on the poorest countries or merely wrapping its old policy in new words? The growing criticism of the IMF in recent years strengthened latterly by the evaluation of the ESAF (Enhanced Structural Adjustment Facility) programmes, which once again proved their blatant weaknesses called for reaction and is now triggering changes real or only rhetorical? There will be no more old-style ESAF loans based on macro-economic structural adjustment programmes. But the credit line remains, and is now called the Poverty Reduction and Growth Facility (PRGF). This will be granted on the basis of the PRSPs, which in each case must also be accepted by the IMF board of directors. How much influence will the IMF have on the design of the PRSPs? What happens if a government choose macro-economic strategies combat poverty which go against previous IMF policy? Open questions. Moreover, there is still no answer to the question of why the IMF is at al coming on with long-term and low-interest lines of credit in the poorest countries.

Mixed Feelings with Regard to World Bank Role

- Will the World Bank use the PRSP process to expand its own institutional power further? NGOs in the North and South are viewing this with mixed feelings. Many welcome the fact that for the moment the World Bank appears to be asserting itself against its twin, the IMF. On the other hand, 50 years of experience with World Bank strategies have certainly not strengthened their trust in the Bank's ability to make a convincing fight against poverty. That is why the EURODAD network also questions the role of the World Bank (and the IMF) in the PRSP process. It says the papers should not be presented to the two financial institutions, whose power over the development strategies of countries of the South thus would increase further. Rather, PRSPs should for example, be laid before a Round Table of all donors chaired by the United Nations Development Programme (UNDP).

Ownership

- The principles of developing countries being responsible for their own development strategies are as old as it is—in theory—right. There have been frequent complaints about shortcomings in ownership. But now, after decades of development strategies being set and structural adjustment programmes being dictated from outside, the governments of the poorest countries, which in many cases have only weak institutional capacities, can hardly taken on sole responsibility overnight. In addition, of course, not a few of the countries are ruled by corrupt political elites (promoted from outside over decades) that give little reason to hope they would immediately switch to poverty reduction politics. Scepticism and critical observation is justified even if there is no alternative to governments of the south taking over greater responsibility.

- Civil society actors are now asked to help out in particular in those countries whose governments appear to be less trustworthy. A nice idea that has little to do with real life. Civil society actors in developing countries in general and in the poorest countries in particular are extraordinarily weak institutions which in many cases are totally dependent on financing from the North.

- The civil society landscape in other countries is even weaker. However, social actors in many countries could make useful contributions to developing sustainable strategies. But that calls for meaningful and lasting support, including financial support, capacity-building, and in some countries also political pressure to gain scope for societal engagement.

It is reasonable that not only the World Bank and other official donors but also, and above all, the northern NGO partners of these actors are now giving much thought to how civil societies in the south can be strengthened.

Participation?

Even assuming there were civil society actors capable of dialogue, that does not clarify what participation in the PRSP process is really supposed to mean. Is civil society only to be listened to, or can it if necessary refuse to approve a PRSP? What impact would have on acceptance of the document by the IMF and World Bank and other donor? And in view of the great time pressure, will civil society be at all able to formulate discuss and feed their positions into the process? It could be of decisive importance for the current debate on the PRSP model to delink the urgently needed debt relief from drawing up a PRSP programme, which simply needs more time. For example, it is conceivable that there would be no great problems in granting a country a moratorium on debt servicing so long as a PRSP process is continuing and then for giving debt when it is completed. That would ease the time problem for NGOs and at the same time maintain pressure on governments actually to arrive at poverty reduction strategies that were developed in a participatory process.

Other Causes of Poverty in Developing Countries

The entire current process is focused on the countries of the south, their governments and societies. That diverts attention from the responsibility of the donors and creditors. Not only that the IMF's structural adjustment programmes to date have been counterproductive for fighting poverty (why does the IMF not admit that openly just for Once?) Not only that the now promised debt reliefs are coming much too late the debt crisis of the poorest countries was deplored decades ago!). The present strategy also ignore various other exogenous causes of poverty in the South. What impacts do the finance and trade policies of northern countries have on the modest attempts to enable sustainable development in the South? What consequences will the continuing cutting of development budgets have on the South (no one anyway ventures to talk nowadays about the old 0.7 per cent ODA-GNP ratio) For the donors and creditors to now pass the buck of sole responsibility to the governments of the South and present themselves in the background as noble do-gooders may be a successful strategy in terms of domestic politics, but not an acceptable one for development policy.

❋❋❋

16

Employment and Promoting Ecology

How a Service Culture Could Put People Back to Work

We are facing two big and urgent social problems: employment and ecology. Both the unemployment of millions of people and the progressive destruction of the ecosphere are alarming. But they are linked with each other. The 'greening' of industrial products, processes and services could provide many more jobs.

Unemployment has many causes, including:

- Sluggish markets;
- Stagnating or declining purchasing power;
- Growing uncertainty about the future at all levels;
- lack of will and/or ability to innovate.

But joblessness is by far due mostly to the high efficiency of industrial machinery, which produces ever more, ever faster, with ever fewer workers.

Waste of Resources

The extremely high productive use of human labour and the extremely low productive use of resources are manifested by gigantic mountains of waste. Already today, the junked cars on scrap heaps alone would form a line that would reach to the moon. The scene is the same with discarded electrical and electronic appliances. Every year, millions of tons of ovens, washing machines, refrigerators, dishwashers, TV sets, entertainment electronics equipment and small appliances are being wasted.

If we throw away all these things after a relatively short time we are not only being wasteful and irresponsible with resources, but equally so with people's work. For with the products and materials we discard, we also dispose of the human labour they contain. It is imperative that we radically reduce the enormous turnovers of material and energy. In other words, the productivity of raw materials and energy must be markedly increased. Specifically, that means we must draw as many services as possible from one kilogram of material or 1 kWh of energy. Reducing the enormous flows of materials into the industrial system, as well as developing cycles of materials and responsibility (the manufacturer taken back and repairing and/or remanufacturing used products and materials) and the main pillars of a sustainable development that can cope with the future.

The industrialized nations must cut their consumption of raw materials by a factor of about 10 by 2050; if they are to be able to handle the challenges of the future. To achieve that reduction, innovation efforts must be directed at increasing resource productivity and/or ecological efficiency. In particular, strategies to extend the useful life of goods and intensify their use could result in reducing both the speed and volume of the flows of resources to industry.

Increasing Resource Productivity

In dealing with nature, we and industry are facing radical change. This is the transition from environmental protection (preservation of nature and health) to greater resource productivity (which at the same time means greater competitiveness). As a rule, environmental protection costs money, while higher resource productivity usually cuts manufacturing costs and/or increases a company's profitability. If the company can sell the same utility or benefits while using fewer resources, it saves twofold: in buying raw materials and on waste disposal. Thereby the rule is that goods and components cycles are more profitable than resources cycles, and that the company which is first in the market gains an additional competitive advantage in terms of a lead in knowledge and image. If a service, or benefits in the form of services, can be sold instead of products, the decoupling of company success and materials flows is even greater.

Impacts on Employment

The two social problem areas of work and ecology have to date been perceived and treated separately in politics, in industry and in our own minds. And, I believe, with little result. The link between the two must be established.

The strategies to boost resource productivity would have considerable impacts on the change in industrial structures, on handling existing product inventories, and on employment. In particular, the strategies would lead to a switch of focal point from a raw materials-intensive and use-value-related service economy. This is where another view of profitability comes in. Business management would no longer focus on value added, but on maintenance of value over longer periods based on the intrinsic value of a product. Expressed as a question, the value factor, which would move to the centre of business thinking and dealing, means: how can the utilisation value be improved and sold? How can products be made with as few raw materials and as little energy as possible and create a high benefit as pollutant-free as possible for as long as possible during their entire life-cycle?

With regard to employment, the production of long-life goods would appear at first sight to lead to a reduction in the need for work. In fact, however, the strategies to increase resources productivity have positive net employment impacts. The reason is that saving resources is based in principle on substituting energy by work, rather than the reverse as has been customary to date.

If the useful life of products is extended, that will not only preserve most of the materials and energy they contain as well as the work invested in them. The products will also require a considerable amount of mostly skilled work input. Reconditioning products is as a rule more labour-intensive than manufacturing them. So large-scale reconditioning and repair work increase the number of skilled jobs and at the same time reduces the inflows of materials and energy.

Comparing a car with a life-cycle of 20 years with two others that each have useful lives of 10 years gives a good example. The first car causes an increase in employment per life-year of about 50 per cent in terms of total work input in manufacture, service, repairs and reconditioning while at the same time reducing the energy consumption by half.

Regionalisation of Industry

Extending product service life would also mean replacing energy and/or capital by skilled work, helping to save money to boot. But not only rising costs of disposal, materials and energy would reduce consumption. Increasing transport costs would also mean that carrying all kinds of freight halfway around the world would make less and less business sense. That would result in ever more products and materials being circulated, reconditioned, and recycled or reduced on a regional basis. In turn, that would create regional jobs, and be more profitable as well as more promotive of technology—not only from ecological aspects.

In addition, a way of doing business which encompassed material and responsibility cycles would no longer differentiate between manufacturing and reconditioning, or between marketing and remarketing. The structure of such an economy would be predominantly decentralised and regionalised so that it could adapt itself to the new cycles. It also would benefit from the greater efficiency of the new working practices.

True, jobs would be lost in the sectors of central production, and raw materials extraction and processing. But at the same time, more and higher-skilled jobs would emerge. These would not only be better qualified jobs, but also decentralized because reconditioning, repairs and maintenance must be done near the customer. And that, in turn, would also reduce goods traffic.

In addition, skilled workers would be needed because in many cases of small production runs it makes sense and is also more economical to hire such people. They can work faster and more flexibly—and mostly cheaper—than fully-automated production lines.

There also would be a growing need for maintenance, repairs and reconditioning. More and more people would be wanted for reconditioning, that is, the remanufacturing of old products. As reconditioning involves far more craft work than highly rationalised new production, there would be a positive impact on the labour market if there were more of the former and correspondingly less of the latter.

From Production to Services

Switching to long-life products and changing from selling products to selling use-values would strengthen the current trend of jobs shifting from industrial production to the service sector. For example, if the service of individual transport were to be sold instead of the product car, the company with the competitive advantage would be the one that had a service centre in every town and village, with appropriately staffed workshops and sales or rental facilities.

Enduring change towards a knowledge-intensive and use-value-related service economy would not only mean that more people would be needed to fill jobs. It would offer more opportunities for part-time work, as well as possibilities of employment for older people and the handicapped. People who earlier could not keep up with the pace of working life would be more inclined to return to it. Another impact would be that many companies would reduce their dependence on the world market. They would no longer switch certain tasks abroad, but assign them to their part-time employees, helping them to meet their commitments as self-employed entrepreneurs.

The latter would be accommodated by an ecology-driven fiscal reform which would make massive cuts or changes in subsidies and raise the cost of energy and raw materials consumption. This move would be accompanied by a reduction in income tax and non-wage costs such as social security contributions. The market would thus be more efficient, energy—and material-intensive new production more expensive, labour-intensive repair work and reconditioning cheaper, and jobs would remain in the home country or region.

A number of more recent studies show clearly that an ecological tax reform would help to create jobs, and thereby could make a decisive contribution to reducing unemployment.

❋❋❋

17

Defining the Singapore Message of WTO

The first two years of the World Trade Organisation have been very encouraging. A few key aspects are as follows:

- One success that stands out above all the rest is the strengthening of the dispute settlement mechanism. This is the heart of the WTO system. Not only has its proved credible and effective in dealing with disputes, it has helped resolve a significant number at the consultation stage. Furthermore, developing countries have become major users of the system, a sign of their confidence in it which was not so apparent under the old system.

- Secondly, the continuing increase in the WTO's membership, emphasizes the vitality of the institution and the multilateral trading system that it embodies. It has now reached 123 members, and there are 30 candidates for accession including some truly major trading partners. It is imperative that it has succeeded in each of these accession negotiations, but in a way which strengthens the system as a whole.

- Thirdly, giving renewed impetus to the completion of critical negotiations towards the multilateral liberalisation in the *financial services* and *telecommunications* is very important. The resolve of the Quad countries is an encouraging sign in this respect. Countries at all levels of development have a vital interest in seeing the best possible outcome in these negotiations. Financial services and basic telecommunications are the arteries and the nervous system of the economy, and their importance to development prospects is crucial.

- Among the issues that are of particular concern to developing countries, one important concern is *textiles*. Developing countries do not want to re-write the Uruguay Round Agreement, but they are concerned to see it implemented fully in spirit as well as in letter—which means doing so in a commercially meaningful way. This is a concern, which must be taken very seriously.

- Last-but certainly not the least, the progress is now being made towards elimination of tariff on *information technology* equipment. They have reached and multilateral agreement in this sector at Singapore have succeeded in unlocking one of the key tools of future growth in industrial and developing countries alike.

These are some of the issues that set the stage for developing the WTO's work programme. This means clarifying the steps to renew negotiations in areas like services and agriculture, which come up at the end of the century. It also means seeing how to approach the commitments which already exist concerning investment, competition policy and government procurement. The immediate task is to build bridges among Members' positions.

Intensive work is beginning to reveal some common ground in a number of areas. For example, the importance of investment, especially for developing countries. Foreign direct investment inflows to developing countries, though their distribution is uneven, increased from an average of about US $22 billion during the second half of the 1980s to about US $100 billion in 1995. And the importance of foreign direct investment goes beyond its mere volume, since it makes available technological, marketing, organisational and managerial inputs to the host country.

The treatment of investment in the multilateral system is still a difficult issue, but there seems to be a broad level of agreement that further work is needed-if not on where it should take place.

The Most Thorny Issue

The most thorny issue is *labour standards,* where the proposals of some Members for work in the WTO have produced clear differences of view. Even here, though, some common ground has been made out in terms of shared principles:

- The respect for core labour standard has been agreed by all Members in the Universal Declaration on Human Rights;
- All delegations have recognised the primary role of the ILO in international labour issues;
- The competitive advantage of low-wage countries has not been called into questions; and
- No one has opposed statements by major proponents of the issue that trade sanctions are not envisaged.

Even on the basis of these elements, it is easy to reach consensus on this issue, but it is vital that it has not become a divisive or disruptive point at Singapore. The key to reach agreement on the WTO's work programme is to understand that the whole political logic of trade has changed. Especially in the newer areas of the trade universe, industrialised and developing countries are on the same side of the table. In areas like financial services, telecommunications or investment, it is not a question of concessions from one side to the other but of a shared interest in agreeing commitments and rules to the common benefit.

Benefits of Globalisation

This change reflects the inescapable reality of global economic integration. Globalisation certainly presents countries with challenges of adjustment—though these are outweighed by the tremendous opportunities it offers. In many countries it is not uncommon to see a defensive reaction to these challenges, one which plays up the supposed threat from developing country imports or industrialised country investment. How to counter this? By emphasising the benefits of globalisation and the interdependence it brings with it. The latest UNCTAD report, for example, shows that the outlook for developing countries is generally brighter than for industrialised countries, and in fact developing countries are now an important source of global growth, on which the prospects of the industrialised world more and more depend. In turn, the developing countries depend on industrialised country markets maintaining and improving their openness.

This is why it is so important that Ministers in Singapore sent a strong political message, one which emphasizes the opportunities in the new global economy, which generally do not receive the same emphasis as the challenges. It is a message which recognises the power of the multilateral system as formidable engine for growth in trade, investment and employment.

It is a message about the vital relationship between the multilateral system and regional trade liberalisation, aimed at reinforcing the m.f.n. principle and ensuring that regional and multilateral system converge around it.

Bold Measures for the Least-Developed

And it is a message of unity among industrial and developing countries, and one of determination to help the least-developed countries come in from the margins through bold and specific measures. This last point is particularly urgent need. An interdependent world means that we are all in the same boat together, and no one can watch with equanimity while the other end of the boat sinks.

The G7 leaders at Lyon wisely made the plight of the least-developed countries a priority, and WTO made a proposal to them. *Its main features are:*

- Full and rapid implementation of the Marrakesh Declaration on the least-developed countries;
- Improving their market access by working towards the elimination of all tariffs and non-tariff barriers on least developed country exports;
- Helping to improve the investment climate they face, especially by creating a more level playing field through negotiating, at the appropriate time, multilateral rules in the WTO;
- Helping to build human and institutional capacity by improving the effectiveness and coordination of technical cooperation. The WTO has made a start in this direction with UNCTAD and the International Trade Centre, and are working hard to improve cooperation with the World Bank and International Monetary Fund. There are especially interesting prospects for extending the reach and the impact of WTO efforts through the use of new information technology, a field where the Bank already has considerable expertise.

One has to encourage a positive consideration of these points inside the WTO and beyond. We have to see a commitment to action along these lines as a very important message of Singapore. In Singapore some of the key questions for global economic development have been on the table. It is essential to reinforce the effort to find the answers together with the partners in the Bank and the Fund.

***

18

Overview of WTO's First Year

An important task facing the WTO is that of making the new multilateral trading system truly global in scope and application. While the present membership accounts for more than 90 per cent of world trade, a number of nations are still outside. Many of them have requested accession to the WTO. Twenty eight governments—ranging from China, the Russian Federation, Ukraine, and Vietnam to the Baltic States, Bulgaria, Mongolia, Panama and Vanuatu are at various stages of a process that has become more involved because of the WTO's increased coverage relative to the GATT. With many of the candidates currently undergoing a process of transition from centrally planned to market economies, accession to the WTO offers these countries—in addition to the usual trade benefits—a way of underpinning their domestic reform processes.

Trade Policy Reviews

The 1995 programme extended the coverage to services, intellectual property and other policies covered by the Uruguay Round agreements. Reviews of developed countries have highlighted the generally open nature of their trade policy regimes for industrial products, coupled with a tendency to protect "sensitive" sectors, such as agriculture, textiles and clothing, and to use contingency protection, both of which impose high costs on the rest of the economy. Reviews of developing and transition economies have underlined the progress of autonomous trade liberalisation and the rapid pace of change to enhance economic efficiency through deregulation, privatisation, and more open investment regimes.

Dispute Settlement

Since 1 January 1995, new disputes follow the procedures of the Dispute Settlement Understanding annexed to the WTO agreement. As is well known, these procedures mark a substantial change from the past. They are a unified set of rules which apply generally to all WTO disputes, the adoption of panel reports cannot be blocked by parties to the dispute, and they provide for the appeal of a panel decision to a new seven-person Appellate Body. The new procedure are overseen by the General Council, sitting as the Dispute Settlement Body.

As of 27 November, the Dispute Settlement Body had been notified of 21 requests for consultation, the step which marks the beginning of a WTO dispute. As these requests by different Members sometimes concerned the same measure, the number of distinct measures subject to disputes was 14. Of these 14, four have been withdrawn, and panels have been established in four.

All cases brought so far have involved goods and GATT 1994. Most of the 21 requests have additionally invoked other goods agreements: Technical Barriers to Trade (seven), Application of Sanitary and Phytosanitary Measures (five), Customs Valuation (three), Agriculture (two), and Licensing (two). In one case the General Agreement on Trade in Services has been invoked.

It is too early to draw definite conclusions on the functioning of the WTO dispute settlement system. The total requests for consultations and panels established are roughly on the same level as during 1994 under the GATT. However the number of disputes (involving different measures) is somewhat less than before in terms of requests for consultation (14 versus 18) and panels established (four versus nine). The parties involved in the disputes are largely unchanged: as before, the United States, the European Communities, Japan and Canada have been the most active participants. Developing countries, however, have been more active as complainants than in the past: Brazil, Chile, Guatemala, Honduras, India, Mexico, Peru, Singapore, Thailand, and Venezuela have been or are all parties to WTO disputes.

Dispute settlement under the GATT 1947 and the Tokyo Agreements. During the review period, dispute actions have been initiated or pursued under certain WTO predecessor agreements still in force. Under the GATT 1947, four panel reports EC-Member states' import regimes for bananas, EC-Import regime for bananas, United States—Restrictions on imports of tuna and United States—Taxes on Automobiles were submitted to the Council for adoption, and there was one new request for consultations (Chile—Taxes on distilled spirits).

Under the Anti-Dumping Agreement, one new panel report was adopted (EC-Anti-dumping duties on imports of cotton yarn from Brazil), and one new panel report was circulated (EC-Anti-dumping duties on audio tapes in cassettes originating in Japan). Under the Subsidies Agreement, one panel case was suspended (United States—Countervailing duties on certain carbon settle flat products from several Member states of the EC), one new panel report circulated (United States—Imposition of countervailing duties on certain hot-rolled lead and bismuth carbon steel products originating in France, Germany and the United Kingdom), and one panel report adopted (United States—Countervailing duties on non-rubber footwear from Brazil).

Balance-of-Payment Restrictions

By the end of 1995, eleven Members will have held consultations, under Articles XII or XVIII: B of the GATT, with the WTO and/or GATT 1947 Committees. In June 1995, the Committees requested Slovakia to eliminate the 1994 import surcharge by the end of 1995, if possible, but in any case before 30 June 1996. Poland was requested to eliminate in import surcharge established in 1992 by the time of the next consultation, due in June 1996. The Committee recommended to Sri Lanka not to have recourse to the provisions or Article XVIII:B. Consultations were also held with Bangladesh and the Philippines, and consultations with India will be held. Egypt, Israel and South Africa disinvoked the BOP provisions, in July, September and November 1995 respectively.

Hungary made a notification prior to the imposition of an import surcharge on 20 March 1995 and consulted with the Committees in June. The Committees requested Hungary to present a concrete timetable for the reduction and elimination of the surcharge. In July, Brazil invoked Article XVIII:B in respect of a quota on imports of motor vehicles for the second half of 1995. Following the Committees request at consultations held in October 1995, the import quota was withdrawn.

Trade and Environment

During the first part of 1995, the new WTO Committee on Trade and Environment (CTE) reviewed the nine items on its work programme. With respect to three items, the CTE was able to take advantage of and build on the work done by the GATT Group on Environmental Measures and International Trade during 1991-93: these were the relationship between WTO provisions and trade measureds taken pursuant to multilateral environmental agreements (MEAs), eco-labelling and packaging requirements, and the transparency of trade-related environmental measures and environment-related trade measures. Regarding exports of domestically prohibited goods, work in the CTE has also been able to benefit from earlier discussions in GATT. With respect to the other five items in its work programme, discussions in the CTE have often involved examining trade issues from new perspectives.

Where the CTE is charged with addressing the relationship between WTO provisions and trade-related environmental measures or trade measures applied for environmental purposes discussions have considered a number of policies, related those policies to relevant WTO provisions, and examined how those provisions apply—including whether they provide adequate rules and disciplines to ensure that unnecessary trade restrictions and distortions are avoided. Some delegations have also emphasised the need for the Committee to consider to what extent WTO provisions adequately accommodate trade and trade-related measures serving environmental purposes, and in this respect one proposal has been made to amend and/or interpret GATT Article XX to clarify its relationship to trade measures taken pursuant to multilateral environmental agreements.

The goal of sustainable development is stated several times in the Marrakesh Ministerial Decision of Trade and Environment. Discussions in the CTE on the effect of environmental measures on market access, especially in relation to developing countries (particularly the least-developed) and the environmental benefits of removing trade restrictions and other distortions have indicated a widespread belief that the complementarities between good environmental policy making and good trade policy-making have a particular potential to promote and accelerate sustainable development. Further liberalisation of trade in goods and in services would allow the same level of output to be produced at less resource cost, generate income that can be used to help pay for environmental protection and conservation, and remove restrictive trade policies that impact adversely on the environment. More broadly, it is evident from the CTE discussions that all believe there is no inherent contradiction between upholding and safeguarding an open, non-discriminatory and equitable multilateral trading system on the one hand, and protecting the environment and promoting sustainable development on the other.

Technical Cooperation and Training

The expanded scope of the WTO has increased substantially the demand for technical assistance. Over sixty national or regional seminars, workshops and technical missions were arranged during 1995. In addition, a total of ninety-nine officials from developing countries and from economies in transition participated in the Trade Policy Courses, covering aspects of trade policy, international trade law and the multilateral trading system. A Workshop on Notification Requirements of the GATT/WTO legal system was held in Geneva, as well as the sixth Special Training Course on Dispute Settlement Procedures and Practices.

Cooperation with Other Organisations

There are two aspects to cooperation between the WTO and other international organisations—the nature of the formal institutional relationships, and the informal cooperative efforts in such as technical assistance and economic research.

As regards the first aspect, An agreement has been concluded with the United Nations, on the basis of Article V of the WTO and in line with the mandate given by Members, that is consistent with the respective status and mandate given by Members, that is consistent with the respective status and mandate of the two organisations (in particular, the contractual nature of the WTO). Under the arrangement, cooperation between the Secretaries will be improved, including new and expanded cooperation between the WTO and United Nations Conference on Trade and Development (UNCTAD).

Another important area of cooperation currently underway or in preparation is the Secretariat's programme of activities for Africa, a results-oriented initiative to help African countries expand and diversify their trade, to be pursued in a strongly cooperative fashion with other intergovernmental organisations, in particular with UNCTAD and ITC.

Future cooperation between the WTO and UNCTAD will not be limited to the WTO programme of activities for Africa. To enhance cooperation between the two organisations and develop further the already strong complementariy. To work for a greater complementary in technical cooperation—not only between the WTO, UNCTAD and the ITC, but also with other agencies, whether in the UN system, the Bretton Woods Organisations, or regional bodies—in order to improve coordination across the board and make better use of resources. If all shows that the WTO's First years performance is upto the expectations.

❋❋❋

19

Overview of WTO's First Two Years

An important task facing the WTO is that of making the new multilateral trading system truly global in scope and application. While the present membership accounts for more than 90 per cent of world trade, a number of nations are still outside. Many of them have requested accession to the WTO. Twenty eight governments—ranging from China, the Russian Federation, Ukraine and Vietnam to the Baltic States, Bulgaria, Mongolia, Panama and Vanuatu are at various stages of a process that has become more involved because of the WTO's increased coverage relative to the GATT. With many of the candidates currently undergoing a process of transition from centrally planned to market economies, accession to the WTO offers these countries—in addition to the usual trade benefits—a way of underpinning their domestic reform processes.

Trade Policy Reviews

The 1995 programme extended the coverage to services, intellectual property and other policies covered by the Uruguay Round agreements. Reviews of developed countries have highlighted the generally open nature of their trade policy regimes for industrial products, coupled with a tendency to protect "sensitive" sectors, such as agriculture, textiles and clothing, and to use contingency protection, both of which impose high costs on the rest of the economy. Reviews of developing and transition economies have underlined the progress of autonomous trade liberalisation and the rapid pace of change to enhance economic efficiency through deregulation, privatisation, and more open investment regimes.

Dispute Settlement

Since January 1, 1995, new dispute follow the procedures of the Dispute Settlement Understanding annexed to the WTO agreement. As is well-known, these procedures mark a substantial change from the past. They are a unified set of rules which apply generally to all WTO disputes, the adoption of panel reports cannot be blocked by parties to the dispute, and they provide for the appeal of a panel decision to a new seven-person Appellate Body. The new procedure are overseen by the General Council, sitting as the Dispute Settlement Body.

As of 27 November, the Dispute Settlement Body had been notified of 21 requests for consultations, the step which marks the beginning of a WTO dispute. As these requests by different members sometimes concerned the same measure, the number of distinct measures subject to disputes was 14. Of these 14, four have been withdrawn, and panels have been established in four.

All cases brought so far have involved goods and GATT 1994. Most of the 21 requests have additionally invoked other goods agreements: Technical Barriers to Trade (seven), Application of Sanitary and Phytosanitary Measures (five), Customs Valuation (three), Agriculture (two), and Licensing (two). In one case the General Agreement on Trade in Services has been invoked.

It is too early to draw definite conclusions on the functioning of the WTO dispute settlement system. The total requests for consultations and panels established are roughly on the same level as during 1994 under the GATT. However the number of disputes (involving different measures) is somewhat less than before in terms of requests for consultation (14 versus 18) and panels established (four versus nine). The parties involved in the disputes are largely unchanged: as before, the United States, the European Communities, Japan and Canada have been the most active participants. Developing countries, however, have been more active as complainants than in the past: Brazil, Chile, Guatemala, Honduras, India, Mexico, Peru, Singapore, Thailand, and Venezuela have been or are all parties to WTO disputes.

Dispute Settlement Under the GATT 1947 and the Tokyo Agreements

During the review period, dispute actions have been initiated or pursued under certain WTO predecessor agreements still in force. Under the GATT 1947, four panel reports EC-Member States' Import Regimes for bananas, EC-Import Regime for Bananas, United States-Restrictions on Imports of Tuna and United States-Taxes on Automobiles) were submitted to the Council for adoption, and there was one new request for consultations (Chile-Taxes on distilled spirits).

Under the Anti-dumping Agreement, one new panel report was adopted (EC-Anti-dumping duties on imports of cotton yarn from Brazil), and one new panel report was circulated (EC-Anti-dumping duties on audio tapes in cassettes originating in Japan). Under the Subsidies Agreement, one panel case was suspended (United States-Countervailing duties on certain carbon steel flat products from several Member states of the EC), one new panel report circulated (United States-Imposition of Countervailing Duties on certain hot-rolled lead and bismuth carbon steel products originating in France, Germany and the United Kingdom), and one panel report adopted (United States-Countervailing Duties on non-rubber footwear from Brazil).

Balance-of-Payment Restrictions

By the end of 1995, eleven Members will have held consultations, under Articles XII or XVIII: B of the GATT, with the WTO and/or GATT 1947 Committees. In June 1995, the Committees requested Slovakia to eliminate the 1994 import surcharge by the end of 1995, if possible, but in any case before June 30, 1996. Poland was requested to eliminate an import surcharge established in 1992 by the time of the next consultation, due in June 1996. The Committee recommended to Sri Lanka not to have recourse to the provisions or Article XVIII:B. Consultations were also held with Bangladesh and the Philippines, and consultations with India will be held. Egypt, Israel and South Africa disinvoked the BOP provisions, in July, September and November 1995 respectively.

Hungary made a notification prior to the imposition of an import surcharge on March 20, 1995 and consulted with the Committees in June. The Committees requested Hungary to present a concrete timetable for the reduction and elimination of the surcharge. In July, Brazil invoked Article XVIII:B in respect of a quota on imports of motor vehicles for the second half of 1995. Following the Committees request at consultations held in October 1995, the import quota was withdrawn.

Trade and Environment

During the first part of 1995, the new WTO Committee on Trade and Environment (CTE) reviewed the nine items on its work programme. With respect to three items, the CTE was able to take advantage of and build on the work done by the GATT Group on Environmental Measures and International Trade during 1991-1993: these were the relationship between WTO provisions and trade measures taken pursuant to multilateral environmental agreements (MEAs), eco-labelling and packaging requirements, and the transparency of trade-related environmental measures and environment-related trade measures. Regarding exports of domestically prohibited goods, work in the CTE has also been able to benefit from earlier discussions in GATT. With respect to the other five items in its work programme, discussions in the CTE have often involved examining trade issues from new perspectives.

Where the CTE is charged with addressing the relationship between WTO provisions and trade-related environmental measures or trade measures applied for environmental purposes, discussions have considered a number of policies, related those policies to relevant WTO provisions, and examined how those provisions apply—including whether they provide adequate rules and disciplines to ensure that unnecessary trade restrictions and distortions are avoided. Some delegations have also emphasised the need for the Committee to consider to what extent WTO provisions adequately accommodate trade and trade-related measures serving environmental purposes, and in this respect one proposal has been made to amend and/or interpret GATT Article XX to clarify its relationship to trade measures taken pursuant to multilateral environmental agreements.

The goal of sustainable development is stated several times in the Marrakesh Ministerial Decision of Trade and Environment. Discussions in the CTE on the effect of environmental measures on market access, especially in relation to developing countries (particularly the least—developed) and the environmental benefits of removing trade restrictions and other distortions have indicated a widespread belief that the complementarities between good environmental policy-making and good trade policy-making have a particular potential to promote and accelerate sustainable development. Further liberalisation of trade in goods and in services would allow the same level of output to be produced at less resource cost, generate income that can be used to help pay for environmental protection and conservation, and remove restrictive trade policies that impact adversely on the environment. More broadly, it is evident from the CTE discussions that all believe there is no inherent contradiction between upholding and safeguarding an open, non-discriminatory and equitable multilateral trading system on the one hand, and protecting the environment and promoting sustainable development on the other.

Technical Cooperation and Training

The expanded scope of the WTO has increased substantially the demand for technical assistance. Over sixty national or regional seminars, workshops and technical missions were arranged during 1995. In addition, a total of ninety-nine officials from developing countries and from economies in transition participated in the Trade Policy Courses, covering aspects of trade policy, international trade law and the multilateral trading system. A Workshop on Notification Requirements of the GATT/WTO legal system was held in Geneva, as well as the sixth Special Training Course on Dispute Settlement Procedures and Practices.

Cooperation with Other Organisations

There are two aspects to cooperation between the WTO and other international organisations—the nature of the formal institutional relationships, and the informal cooperative efforts in such as technical assistance and economic research.

As regards the first aspect, an arrangement has been concluded with the United Nations, on the basis of Article V of the WTO and in line with the mandate given by Members, that is consistent with the respective status and mandate of the two organisations (in particular, the contractual nature of the WTO). Under the arrangement, cooperation between the Secretaries will be improved, including new and expanded cooperation between the WTO and United Nations Conference on Trade and Development (UNCTAD).

Another important area of cooperation currently underway or in preparation is the Secretariat's programme of activities for Africa, a result-oriented initiative to help African countries expanded and diversify their trade, to be pursued in a strongly cooperative fashion with other inter-governmental organisations, in particular with UNTCAD and ITC.

Future cooperation between the WTO and UNCTAD will not be limited to the WTO programme of activities for Africa. To enhance cooperation between the two organisations and develop further the already strong complementary. To work for a greater complementary in technical cooperation—not only between the WTO, UNCTAD and the ITC, but also with other agencies, whether in the UN system, the Bretton Woods organisations, or regional bodies—in order to improve coordination across the board and make better use of resources. If all shows that the WTO's First years performance is upto the expectations.

World Trade Expanded Strongly in 1995, for the Second Consecutive Year

The volume of world merchandise exports rose by a healthy 8 per cent in 1995—down from 9½ per cent the previous year—while the combined value of cross border trade in goods and services broke the $6,000 billion mark for the first time. Volume growth, in 1996, for merchandise exports is expected to slow modestly but still maintain a robust level around 7 per cent.

Other Highlights

- For the sixth consecutive year, trade growth exceeded output growth by a wide margin.
- Among the recently-identified factors behind this trend is the rapid expansion in non-OECD countries of processing trade (assembly of manufactures under special tariff regimes, involving imported components and materials, often in designated export processing zones).
- For the fourth consecutive year Asia's import growth exceeded its export growth.
- Central and Eastern Europe was the most dynamic region for trade, with export and import values up by at least one-quarter.
- Trade in office and telecom equipment—which now exceeds trade in agricultural products of trade in mining products—was again the most dynamic category of manufactures trade.
- Africa and the Middle East recorded their best trade performances in recent years, as exports or mining

products picked-up strongly mainly due to higher prices for fuels and non-ferrous metals.

- In value terms, world trade in commercial services increased 14 per cent last year, compared with a 19 per cent increase for merchandise trade. Exports of "other private services"—such as insurance, banking and telecommunications—out-performed exports of tourism and transportation services.

❋ ❋ ❋

20

Can Economic Growth Reduce Poverty?

New Findings on Inequality, Economic Growth and Poverty

Many people still think first of 'economic growth' in relation to poverty reduction. Indeed, their correlation is one of the most-discussed issues of combating poverty. The relationship is of great importance because if there is a clear causal dependency, reducing poverty could fundamentally be limited to measures to promote growth. However, if there was low growth or stagnation it would not be possible to reduce poverty decisively. In the opposite case, that of the phenomena having no causal relation, promising measures to reduce poverty could be taken up even without economic growth.

Hardly anyone now explicitly expresses the view that economic development trickles down automatically to the poor. Practical experience has refuted this assumption dating from the early days of development policy in the 1960s. However, a number of studies show development of growth and a decline in poverty running parallel. On the other hand, there are also examples which show that despite high economic growth, poverty is not reduced markedly. The common answer to the question this raises is thus: Yes, growth can reduce poverty, but only if additional measures oriented on the poor are taken up. This is often termed pro-poor-growth. But what that means in detail, and whether economic growth as such plays a causal role at all, is not clarified. It is worth taking a look at the arguments on the basis of more recent empirical and theoretical knowledge.

No Direct Causality Between Growth and Poverty Reduction

Among the many indicators of poverty, the income of the poor (income poverty) has the closest relationship to economic growth. An increase in gross domestic product and thus national income could, if other factors come into play be linked with an increase in the per capita income of the poor.

Such a relationship between economic growth and the income of the poor, however, cannot be described as causal, as is asserted implicitly time and again by the statement that growth is a necessary but not sufficient precondition for poverty reduction. Insofar as growth and poverty reduction arise at the same time at the end of a process, they exist alongside each other. It would be almost a tautology to say that the former is the cause or part-cause of the latter Both express the same thing, namely a change in per capita income as well, and both have similar causes. What matters is recognising what these causes are and what specific factors must come into play so that the income of the poor grows too. Growth as a "prerequisite" or "condition" is then no longer the focus; the priority is asking for specific policies that result in higher incomes for the poor. The detour in thinking about growth is not necessary. Since, however, it is based on similar factors, such as fiscal policy/budget structure, employment policy, combating inflation, and institutional development, economic growth can also emerge if poverty is reduced. The difference of views lies in the fact that under the heading 'poverty reduction' the aim is no longer growth, but a purposeful reduction of poverty.

Therefore, in reverse, successful combating of poverty can be seen as being the cause of growth insofar as activating the capabilities of the poor and using their productive capacity of the poor and using their productive capacity triggers economic drive.

Indirect Causality Between Growth and Poverty Reduction?

So even if economic growth fundamentally has no direct causal impact on poverty, growth still can reduce it indirectly.

This is the case when due to positive economic development a government has greater revenue and uses the surplus for combating poverty, for example by providing such public goods as education and health services. Also in these cases, however, growth is not a compelling precondition. Even without growth greater government revenue can be achieved for example by more efficient tax collection. And leeway for social welfare spending can be gained by redistributing the budget, such as by cutting military appropriations. Furthermore, an automatic process is not given because the government can also use surplus funds for non-social purposes.

Creation of jobs due to increased economic activity can be another indirect link between economic growth and income poverty, if such a development generates income and reduces poverty. But also in this case I see no compelling causality because, for instance, industrial jobs are not necessarily open to the really poor. In addition, these positive impacts occur to a considerable extent only in the event of labour-intensive development. In many countries, however, economic growth is achieved by capital-intensive production.

Inequality, Growth and Income Poverty

If national incomes, grow, a naïve observer might assume that the income of the poor must also grow along with it. But that would be a statistical fallacy. Even if only the income of the rich grows, this results in macro-economic statistics showing a higher per capita income. What the true conditions are is shown as soon as one divides the population statistically into income groups, such as in fifths, as is usual. It then turns out that the bald figures on average per capita growth can certainly cloak a situation where the income of the richest fifth of the population is growing fast while that of the poorest fifth is stagnating. Despite growth, the gap between the two becomes even wider.

The unequal distribution of income (and of other assets such as property and access to social services), and its connection to poverty reduction and growth has recently returned to the forefront of the debate.

It is obvious that inequality and its changes have direct effects on the poverty situation. Does inequality also have an impact on poverty via its relation to growth, because growth promotes or reduces inequality? Earlier, the predominant view was that rapid growth was linked with at least a temporary increase in inequality, so that a distinct policy of growth initially disadvantaged the poor.

The current dominant view is that growth has no foreseeable effects on inequality and that inequality changes only very slowly, in reverse, however, it is assumed that greater equality is a determinant of growth. According to that view, an indirect relationship between poverty on one side and inequality as a factor dependent upon growth on the other is not given.

That leads to the conclusion that fair distribution has more weight than growth. Fair distribution, however, does not depend upon growth. An appropriate policy is possible at any time, not only after an economic situation has improved. The notion that still shimmers through the debate that "something must be earned first before it can be distributed", is wrong. It is a matter of designing policy and the entire economic process right from the start in such a way that the surplus benefits all including the poor. Important elements of such a policy are, for example, land reform and development of finance systems.

Relationship of Growth to Poverty

According to today's conventional wisdom, income poverty expresses only a part of what poverty means. Not least through the voices of the poor themselves, it has become clear that violation of human dignity and rights, a lack of participation in decisions and exclusion from society, unequal treatment of men and women, and vulnerability are also regarded as poverty. For poverty is caused to a great degree by conflicts of power and interests. Income poverty often is not even seen as the greatest problem.

What relationship do these more far reaching characteristics of poverty have to economic growth? A direct relationship of growth to socially-related aspects such as women's inheritance rights, land rights and exclusion from decisions cannot be seen. Considerable improvements in favour of the poor can be achieved here even without economic growth.

Those who see a strong and causal connection between economic growth and poverty reduction must ask themselves what the prospects are for high growth rates and thus for a decline in poverty. Coupling poverty reduction to economic growth is problematic. If only low growth rates are to be expected.

Another question is whether continuous increases in growth are at all desirable and possible in the medium to long term. In this connection, a difference should perhaps be made between developing countries and industrialised nations. But environmental compatibility and availability of resources set limits to growth for both. Some academics assume that industrialised nations have already reached an inherent limit (stagnation theory) and that the high growth rates of earlier years will not return. Moreover, they add, full employment is no longer achievable due to, among other things, an ongoing increase in productivity, and current unemployment cannot be reduced by customary means. In any case, if growth were to be taken as the major benchmark, the prospects for a radical reduction of income poverty around the world would be modest.

Summing Up

Poverty is a complex problem and reducing it depends upon many interconnected factors that is why poverty cannot be attributed to one main cause nor its reduction based on one main strategy. Economic growth is just one strategic element among many others related to poverty reduction. An indirect causal connection between growth and poverty reduction can only be seen because governments will have a grater scope for action due to economic growth, and if they promote labour-intensive development.

Therefore growth's role in poverty reduction must be put into perspective growth cannot be the first thing that comes to mind, nor is it the golden path to reducing poverty. The simplistic theory of economic growth as the main condition obstructs the bigger picture; it clings to the underlying and ongoing belief in the trickle-down effect. Even if there is no growth or for inherent reasons there can be none, there are promising ways to take on the challenge of mass poverty in the developing countries. Up front, governments and bilateral and multilateral donors must have the political will to design economic, financial and social policies so that they are oriented on poverty in a coherent way—the result can also be economic growth.

21

Challenging Traditional Economic Growth

Today, saving the planet is about redefining our economic development models. Stirving towards the fulfilment of basic human rights is an integral part of environmental protection. Without a people-centred development strategy we will fail. Conflicting interests and lack of vision and courage are among the many reasons why it is so hard to meet needs in a world of plenty. We are faced with three major challenges in the 1990s:

- To curb population growth and poverty;
- To search for sustainable production and consumption patterns;
- To promote equity.

Population growth is often associated with poverty. But who causes the major strain on the environment? The 1.2 billion poorest people consume small amounts of the world's resources and contribute little to harmful emissions. They do not cause a heavy burden. The day-to-day struggle for survival of the poorest does, however, undermine their resources, and this causes deaths as population grows beyond the carrying capacity of nature. Here two key elements are essential: to turn from non-renewable to renewable resources, and to minimize use of resources through resource efficiency. We must single out the products and processes that must be phased out and those which may be allowed to expand. Right prices that include the ecological costs will be explored further, together with administrative measures. We are ready to examine the possibilities of using "green tax" reforms to enhance employment and harness pollution and inefficient resources use. By shifting the burden of taxes from labour to environmentally harmful products and processes we might achieve a double benefit.

Transport, waste management, energy and land use are obvious areas that need to be affected by policy changes. Individuals must use their power as green-conscious citizens and shoppers—but, in the end, producers and service providers hold the main key to practical action.

The market must be harnessed to meet people's needs both for present and future generations—starting by making economic policies play by the rules of nature. The World Trade Organisation (WTO) negotiations have provided us with instruments to regulate world trade.

Getting the Prices Right

Car emissions may be cut drastically, but the rapid increase of new cars nullifies the benefits. Even the most ardent technological optimist must admit that we need new priorities or cuts in some products and services. For example, we must improve public transport and resource-efficient cars—and reduce traffic.

Traditional economic growth models fall short of solving the problem of unemployment. Indeed, 'robots' and wasteful resource use replace people. There are great job-creating possibilities in environment-friendly produces and processes. Striving towards equity within and between nations, and within and between generations, is the major challenge of our time.

The fact that 20 per cent of the world's population consumes 80 per cent of the world's resources has too long been seen as mainly an ethical challenge. Ethics are not easily translated into politics, especially when confronted with economic and market realities. As equity gradually becomes a security issue—as it will, if we do not bridge the gaps within and between nations—it will climb to the top of the political agenda.

Many of the main conflict areas of today are battlefields of resource management. These will expand greatly if we do not turn conference statements of good intention into action. The 30 year old commitment of the rich countries to meet the target of 0.7 per cent of GNP in official Development Assistance remains unmet.

Two hundred years of Western-led development optimism reached its peak in the late 1980s. When the Berlin wall fell, the economic growth models of the rich countries had become the universal recipe. But as more and more people aspire to join the ranks of the middle classes, the resulting environmental stress calls for a halt, or a radical change of course.

The call for new patterns of production and consumption challenges our traditional concepts of economic growth and the focus on materialism in our culture. Neither the industrialised nor the poorer countries are strangers to radical process of change, though the reasons for change are shifting. And we are truly facing challenging and conflict-provoking changes.

No nation by itself can solve the problems we face. Pollution knows no frontiers, but comes to us with the winds and waves. We have become more and more interdependent. If we are to attain sustainable development, we must commit ourselves through international agreements, through an international rule of law, through the development of financial mechanisms and through institutional agreements. We must develop means and tools to enhance collective security and mutual interests.

***

22

Migration and Development

Migration and development is a growing area of interest. There has been much debate on the negative impacts of migration on development and vice-versa. On the one hand, it is argued that underdevelopment is a cause of migration, and on the other that migration causes developing countries to lose their highly skilled nationals.

While there is a measure of truth in each of these assertions, properly managed international migration holds enormous potential for the development of countries. Remittances have become a prominent source of external funding for developing countries that surpass official development assistance. In 2005, over US $100 billion were sent home in remittances by migrants, helping to sustain the economies of many developing countries. The total amount of resource remitted may even be two or three times higher, since a large number of transactions are carried out through informal channels. Migration can thus contribute to the reduction of poverty at the local and national level, and to a reduction in the economic vulnerability of developing countries.

Migration may be detrimental to the community of origin if the labour market is depleted by the departure of its most productive and/or qualified members ("brain drain"). However, migrants who have developed and improved their skills abroad can be actors of the "brain gain" by transferring and infusing knowledge, skills and technology into their countries, of origin.

In addition, remittances sent home by migrants can be used to sustain development . The Challenge is to develop mechanisms to mitigate as much as possible the negative effects of "brain drain" and to encourage the return of qualified nationals resulting "brain gain".

It should also be noted that in a globalized world, migration is increasingly circular. While many migrants still make a permanent move with their families, an increasing proportion of migratory movements are temporary in nature. Increasingly, countries of origin expect migrants to maintain financial, cultural and sometimes political links with their home country, which may be difficult to reconcile with the expectation for migrants to integrate, on the part of the host country.

In order to benefit from remittances, skills transfer and investment opportunities, it is necessary to create and maintain links between migrants and their potential by encouraging them to contribute human and financial capital to the development of their home communities.

Through advances in communications technology and the decline in travel costs, globalisation has made it easier for migrants to stay in contact with their country of origin and to establish lasting links with diasporas and transnational networks.

In the past, states and the international community formulated and implemented separate policies on poverty reduction, globalisation, security, refugees and migration, with sometimes different or even conflicting objectives.

Better results can be achieved by considering the close interrelationship between migration and development on national and international levels through coherent and coordinated development and migration polices, and between humanitarian assistance and development assistance. Migration polices dealing with the migration-development nexus include facilitating voluntary return and reintegration, either temporary or permanent, particularly of the highly skilled. Other policies address the transfer of remittances, the reduction of transfer costs and investment in the country of origin by diasporas and returning migrants.

It is also necessary to promote and enhance dialogue and cooperation and the national level between different government agencies as well as at the international level. The aim is to ensure that migration contributes to sustainable development, and that in turn development endeavours to contribute to the management of migration.

In recent years, migration has been making its way steadily to the top of the international agenda, and now calls insistently and urgently for the attention of all governments, regard less of their past involvement or interest in the management of migratory processes.

Migratory flows today are more diverse and complex, with more temporary and circular migration. World demographics, economic, political and social trends mean that governments and societies will need to put more emphasis on migration management in all of its dimensions.

If properly managed, migration can be beneficial for all states and societies. If left unmanaged, it can lead to the exploitation of individual migrations, particularly through human trafficking and migrant smuggling, and be a source of social tension, insecurity and bad relations between nations.

Effective management is required to maximise the positive effects of migration and minimise potentially negative consequences. It is essential to establish orderly and safe migration opportunities while ensuring respect for the integrity of national, sovereign borders. Migration management strategies need to result in the implementation of policies; laws and regulations that take into account the rights and obligations of migrations as well as the social and economic interests of nations and responsibilities of governments.

Over the past decades governments have tended to focus on isolated elements of migration and have thus developed ad-hoc strategies to protect their interests. For some, labour migration needs have predominated, for others asylum has been the main concern. However, to be effective, migration management strategies need to address migration in a comprehensive manner. Governments over the past decades have tended to focus on isolated elements of migration. The challenge today is to shift from an isolate and largely in effective focus to more meaningful, constructive and comprehensive approaches.

At the same time, it is necessary to identify, define and address the fundamental policy issues in the migration debates. This is a tall. assignment, since the migratory landscape is complex and rapidly evolving, with challenges emerging at every step of the way.

Most governments are just beginning to develop coherent and comprehensive migration management strategies. There is still a need to better understand migration interests and priorities and to develop a common migration language. Regular dialogue between governments that allows an exchange of experience and the development of new initiatives and approaches to migration management is therefore essential.

***

23

Development

The People Know Best

Meetings of the World Bank and the World Trade Organisation has inspired high-mined protest and, on occasion, even vandalism. But this protest and vandalism may miss the point. It is hard to blame those who complain of bullying or blundering by the great institutions of global power. But the poor of the world, especially the poor of developing countries, deserve more than street demonstrations. The poor understand better than anybody the complicated details of their own poverty—the absence of health care, the lack of education, and all the sinister perils to their own safety and well-being. They know the failures of their governments, and of international institutions.

And that is the point: It is the people of the poor countries who will have to apply new knowledge to design and achieve their own development. A country can only develop when its citizens have the freedom to address their own development problems. The obligation of the rich countries, is to give help where they can. And anyone who doesn't see a moral imperative to contribute to a fairer, more prosperous future is free to frame the obligation differently—as self interest, for example. It will surely serve us better to invest in a peaceful and contented global community than to invite the strife and poverty of unanswered injustice and economic ruin.

Among our relevant conclusions: Powerful institutions of global finance and trade (not least, the World Bank and the World Trade Organisation) can be a source of real promise to poor countries. If governed right, they can help integrate developing economies into the enriching opportunities of global trade and investment. But such promise is often wasted because the very poverty of poor-country governments weakens their ability to negotiate the terms that would serve them best.

Communities in poor countries find themselves at a special disadvantage when it comes to bargaining with foreign investors. Investment can bring growth and spread wealth. It can also threaten human rights and social cohesion, or cultural integrity, and the fragile balance of ecosystems. Nobel economist Amartyasen has spoken powerfully about the intimate relation between development and choice, the subject of his thought-provoking book *Development as Freedom*. Development, Sen argues, "consists of the removal of various types of unfreedoms that leave people with little choice and little opportunity..." He defines freedom as "both the primary end and the principal means of development."

A precondition of this freedom is knowledge—knowledge of the hard facts and the hard science, on which real choices are constructed. Also it is knowledge of good governance—procedures of choice that are effective, responsive and democratic. For budgetary reasons, rich countries contribution in international development was severely cut in the 1990s. Now, along with others in the rich countries, they have to begin to reinvest in international development.

This means a new commitment to the improvement of lives, and to the future that the North must share with the South. It will be a reinvestment in peace, and in our own prosperity. This remains a matter of obligation, and of sensible self-interest.

***

24

Technological Entrepreneurship

The New Force for Economic Growth

Entrepreneurship has emerged as a major new force for change. The dynamic role of modern small business in economic growth has received fresh recognition worldwide. It is essential to promote entrepreneurship and to mobilize the dynamism of the private sector for accelerated national development. An unbridled private sector may not, however, ensure growth with equity. It is the prime responsibility of governments to create policy frameworks that enable business to apply technology for competitive advantage and for the well-being of the public.

The Changing Global Environment

As agents of change and progress, entrepreneurs start by identifying a market opportunity and matching this with social or technical innovations. They then proceed to mobilize the resources necessary to drive their business concept to its commercial realisation. The development of a product or service with a high-technology content—never easy anywhere, or at today's rapidly-changing global environment. It calls for restructuring the available technology and business development systems and developing the skills needed by a new breed of "techno-entrepreneurs" to transform innovations into market opportunities at home and abroad. It also requires reorienting the present processes and priorities of technical and economic cooperation among countries.

Amidst the global concerns of environmental preservation, poverty elimination and social development, the practical problems of entrepreneurship are not being properly addressed, even though entrepreneurs will create the bulk of enterprises, jobs and wealth.

A torrent of technology-based goods hits the market every week, ostensibly improving the quality of our lives while simultaneously creating complexity and dislocation. The pace of progress in information technologies, microelectronics, robotics, new materials, biomedical sciences, space science and other advanced technologies quickens, significantly changing the way we live. The growth of markets for these technologies also proceeds apace.

Further, technological change is taking place today against a background of growing intra-national and international disequilibria. While the transformation from State-centred to market-oriented development is opening up enormous opportunities and options, it has also caused severe short-term hardships. In order to survive and prosper in these changing times, India and its enterprises need enlightened government policies, good technical infrastructure and strong cultural roots.

Traditional production factors are giving way to a new paradigm characterised by new patterns of trade, investment and employment, and by informal networking life-long learning and technological entrepreneurship. The manufacturing sector in India continues to be dominated by food products, textiles, chemicals and other traditional industry, mainly in the public sector. However, change is coming, albeit slowly. State enterprises are being corporatised pending privatisation, and the share of knowledge-based and information-related activities in the marketplace is rising perceptibly. Restructuring policies now place emphasis (often purely rhetorical) on the role of the private sector. The legacy of decades of centrally-planned development is generally inimical to private enterprise. In turn, the private sector has been slow to respond to economic liberalisation in India and generally failed to generate the new employment necessary to absorb new entrants to the labour force.

The regulatory problems of an onerous tax structure and administration, poor access to finance and raw materials, over-regulation of labour and land use, pervasive bureaucracy and restricted markets have been significant barriers to entrepreneurial growth.

Towards Competitive Performance

The imperative of improved performance has serious implications for India if it is to survive, stay abreast and succeed. It calls for national efforts on systemic efficiency and productivity growth, the move from an investment-driven to an innovation-driven economy and sustained higher-order competitiveness; towards enhanced customer satisfaction at home and penetration of selected markets abroad. Concurrently, governments and business have to address such intractable problems as poverty, corruption and the degradation of the environment.

Creating New Technology-Based Ventures

Starting a new business in India is a hazardous task. Problems are compounded when the venture is technology-based:

- Capital requirements are generally larger, while traditional banks are ill-equipped to process the perceived risk. Venture capital generally only becomes an option when the venture has documented the merits of its management, market and innovation.
- Knowledge-based ventures can benefit from linkages to sources of knowledge—e.g. the technical university or research lab. Such mentoring needs to be cultivated.
- Techno-entrepreneurs often have technical skills but usually lack the business management and

marketing skills necessary for success. These need to be supplemented.

- In fields where technology is changing rapidly, it is often advantageous to make technology-acquisition arrangements. Sourcing such innovations, negotiating technology licensing agreements and protecting the intellectual property itself require special skills.
- Knowledge-based innovations are inherently more risky than others. The management of this unique risk requires assessment techniques and vision.
- Technology-based ventures often have social and environmental implications, which need to be managed carefully.
- Penetrating a competitive market requires good market intelligence, a good strategic plan and good luck.

Special Characteristics of "Techno-entrepreneurs"

The popular misconceptions are that techno-entrepreneurs are born, not made; that they take risks with other people's money and fail more often than they succeed. In fact, entrepreneur skills can be identified and developed. The entrepreneur is typically an innovator who formulates new solutions to existing problems; mobilizes resources and stimulates others to participate in his or her team. These aptitudes develop over time, often starting in childhood, as the person faces new challenges and learns from failure.

Entrepreneurial opportunities can be found in every industrializing country, community and family. Principal sources of entrepreneurs for knowledge-based ventures are often the university and government research laboratories, the large industrial and military establishments and professional service firms. Some motivations of the entrepreneur are the need to: be independent; create value; contribute to society; earn recognition; become rich or; quite often, simply not to be unemployed. Value-adding ventures with good growth potential can best be developed in an open market and in a culture which supports risk-taking.

The techno-entrepreneur anywhere has the challenge of moving a concept through the prototype and production phases towards creation of a product which meets market needs at a price consistent with the value created and with the ability of customers to pay.

Equally important, the market itself has to be developed and sustained. It is not enough to be first with a better mousetrap if one does not have the skills to educate and reach potential buyers and to set the market standard.

Hence one has to distinguish between innovators and inventors. The inventor is typically a creative person in a quest for knowledge or for producing new products, without determining in advance whether a real market exists for his or her inventions. On the other hand, the innovator draws on existing knowledge and the talents of others to develop or adapt a product or service at a volume and cost that can capture a significant portion of an identified market. The flexibility and creativity of a small entrepreneurial techno-venture may lead to more incremental and break through innovations than can be generated by larger-sized firms in many sectors.

The pace and pattern of India's economic development now depend in large measure on its technical resource base. In this context, the key determinants are the skills to apply technology for enhanced competitiveness, as well as to create techbased ventures. Techno-entrepreneurs have to be supported by appropriate national structures and international linkages if they are to survive and flourish in an intensely competitive world.

❋❋❋

25

Crisis and New Orientation of Development Policy

The poverty in the South, the dislocations in the East, and the orientation crisis in the North are not isolated phenomena. Rather, they represent an alarming amalgamation of dangers that are globally interlinked.

The low effectiveness of international economic and development policy is rooted in two outdated paradigms on which the present worldwide strategy of economic development is based, namely that:

1. The Western social and economic model optimizes the activation of productive forces—independent of the development stage of a country and its culture and therefore is best suited to satisfy basic needs.
2. It is possible to launch the development of a society from the outside within a few decades—without regard to is cultural and historical background—through external input of money, goods, technology, expertise, and personnel.

The twin paradigms of the timelessness and transferability combined with cultural ecological, and financial restrictions have led international cooperation and development down the wrong path.

Only if we acknowledge the true dimensions of the global dangers, if we recognize the limitations and shortcomings of existing political instruments, and identify outdated theories and contradictory special interests, can we outline the cornerstones of a new policy of global cooperation.

Cornerstones of a New Development Policy

Starting with critical review of the shortcomings and paradigms of the prevailing development strategy, the following ten cornerstones of a new development policy are offered for discussion:

1. Broaden the Concept of Development

Whether a society is considered developed depends on the size of its percapita Gross National Product (GNP). Accordingly, the world is divided into a developed, semi-developed, and underdeveloped world. The yardstick for development, which has become the norm in the industrial countries, is one-dimensional: It only measures the monetary value of goods and services that are exchanged in the marketplace. This standard is too narrow economically because it compresses the multitude and complexity of cultural, societal, historical. social, and human values into a single economic category.

At the most, there can and should be agreement on what development and progress should not bring about: Inability to find enough work to meet the most basic needs; exploitation and oppression of people; loss of cultural wealth and institutions; destruction of natural resources. These, however, are the very values that are sacrificed by the prevailing development strategy. In the future, development policy must do all it can to stop the loss of skills and self-reliance, the plunder of natural resources, the erosion of cultural values, the violation of human dignity and human rights. Initiatives must prevail which are orientated on these values, and not just on the GNP.

2. Concentrate Development Strategy on the Internal Potential of Developing Countries

There must be an end to the manic fixation of development strategy on external inputs and external markets. A new development policy must, above all, improve internal conditions for a productive economy, promote domestic production factors on a broad basis, protect cultural and natural resources, and greatly increase the domestic supply of basic goods. Wherever external inputs are unavoidable, credits must be strictly tied to the productivity and the ability of a country to absorb transfers. External transfers should be concentrated on "Software" for health, education, social participation administative, and legal jurisdiction. Such an approach could also promote training and indigenous technologies, which are so important for economic development.

The set-up and expansion of the productive sectors must be decided, planned, and implemented by the developing countries themselves, and they must assume full responsibility. The external pressures, which force the developing countries into full integration with the world market, must be removed. This presupposes a structural reduction of interest rates.

3. *Make Development Policy a Central Feature of Politics*

Development policy must take the lead in mobilizing the various political forces and government departments to join the fight against the growing global dangers. It must ensure that the actions of all political departments are compatible with development policy is possible only if it becomes the central task of all political sectors, comparable to social and environmental policies, and the central goal of all policies. If development policy is to become a central task, development problems must become a priority in parliament and government. Society must understand that it is in the national interest to accept great global responsibilities.

4. *Reform the World Economy*

The industrial countries must abolish their protectionism in agriculture as well the processed goods sector. Simultaneously, the developing countries need to be protected selectively and for a limited time against imports from the industrial countries. The undifferentiated structural adjustment policies imposed by the IMF must be revised. The trend toward regionalization of the world economy should not be opposed; rather, in the interest of both South and East, it must be regulated constructively to form a new, regionally based world trade structure.

A reform of the international finance system is urgently needed: Interest and exchange rates should not mirror the national interests of the big industrial states and the special interests of large banks and venture capital. Rather, they must reflect the global interest in monetary stability lower and stable interest rates, and sufficient development financing.

However, strengthening the international financial institutions is in the global interest only if the countries of the southern and eastern hemispheres are allowed to exert some influence. An international financial court must guarantee that violations of strict regulations to ensure international stability and solvency can be protested in a court of law.

5. *Redesign the Industrial Society*

As a global social and environmental policy, the new development policy must induce the industrial countries to give up their excessive consumption of air, water, soil, resources, and space. Increased utilization of energy-conservation measures and environmentally friendly technologies is overdue. The economic and social policies of the industrial nations must promote balance rather than growth. This requires radical changes in traditional economic thinking, habits, structures and processes.

In view of limited world resources, unsatisfied existential needs in South and East, and continuous population growth in the South, the only premise for the future can be: Growth rates in the South must be higher than in the North, but they should no longer be in the North, but they should no longer be induced primarily by growth in the North. If economic policies continue to call for the North to provide the locomotive, the North will have to continue to acquire more resources than the South.

The North must relinquish the remaining growth frontiers to the South and East. The South must use this opportunity to activate its internal dynamic potential rather than integrate its economy with the North. However, ecological and social controls must be established at a much earlier stage than was the case in Europe.

6. *Strengthen Development Cooperation*

The share of official development assistance as a percentage of GNP, which dropped from 0.48 per cent in 1982 to 0.34 per cent in 1995 must be gradually raised again and reach at least 0.7 per cent in the year 2000—a goal which OECD established as early as two decades ago and which was reconfirmed at the Rio Earth Summit.

However, we must not succumb to the illusion that a doubling of ODA funds will even remotely meet the financial needs of South and East. State development policy must use its scarce public funds more effectively in the future. It must use restraint whenever partners in the developing countries can accomplish a task on their own and private initiatives and private enterprise are more competent to do the job. The government should be directly engaged only when it can be relatively more productive. Otherwise, it should limit itself to subsidizing private organizations.

7. *New Orientation for Development Cooperation*

The state and its implementation agencies must abandon all direct responsibility for any projects which require unbureaucratic action, economic efficiency, and long-term productivity. It must make a much greater effort to involve NGO's and private venture capital in development projects. At the same time, the state must insist and guarantee that private actions are compatible with social and ecological concerns.

In the future, the main thrust of government projects should be the promotion of the internal potential of a country. This comprises the political and administrative framework conditions of a humane, socially and ecologically sound development: Constitutional government, social institutions which facilitate broad participation of the population in politics, society, and economy; efficient savings, credit, fiscal and financial systems; mechanisms for income, property, and land distribution which promote productivity, justice, and social peace. In addition of this "software" of development, the following is needed: A regimen for the protection of resources and environment; measures to prevent the short-term sell out of natural resources; elementary and general education and training, health care and social safety nets; capacities to develop science and technology.

8. *Reduce the Debt Service and Activate Private Capital*

Public funds must be used to a greater degree for the financial rehabilitation of highly indebted countries in South and East; external demands for interest and principal payments must be adapted to the economic capacity of the respective country and its ability to execute external capital transfers.

Within the framework of international insolvency regulations, initiatives must be developed as a condition for the continuance of the present rules for write-offs which ensure effective cooperation from the banks and alleviate the heavy burden of private credits, with their high interest rates.

State development policy and private business interests should supplement each other. Government promotion of private enterprise initiatives for exports, investment, and employment in the developing countries must take into account their compatibility with development. In reverse, private engagements which effectively promote development must be actively supported by the government. A separate line item must be established in the development budget for such activation of private capital.

9. *Set Regional Priorities*

State development cooperation has been scattering its scarce funds not only among too many sectors, but also among too many partners. In the future, public funds must be concentrated regionally. More emphasis must be placed on regional programs, and development cooperation with threshold countries must be enhanced. A portion of public funds should be set aside to provide an incentive for be set aside to provide an incentive for threshold countries to assist the poorer nations in their own region as well as deal with poverty in their own country.

The new development policy could then also help lessen ethnic-national conflicts and promote peace by sponsoring regional cooperation in joint development projects. For this purpose, regional development funds must be set up for cooperation in the transportation, energy, trade, and finance sectors and last, but not least for regional security systems and disarmament. Such regional funds could also provide the means to project refugees and improve their prospects for an eventual return to their homelands.

❋❋❋

26

Aid Effectiveness as a Multi-level Process

Parallel to the widespread decrease of aid resources provided by donor countries to developing countries in recent years, debate and research on how to make aid more effective has become a major concern of policy-makers and donor aid administrators. Usually, it is suggested that decades of development assistance have at best produced marginal results in terms of improving development levels in the South. Little mention is made of donor's policy shortcomings and the negative impact of these on efforts aimed at reforming and redefining development cooperation in order to enhance aid effectiveness. The policy parameters and operating frameworks of existing aid policies continue to inhibit higher degrees of aid effectiveness. In many donor countries, opinion polls indicate waning public support for development aid.

Increasingly, the moral case for aid is called into question and deeper world market integration tends to be seen as the panacea to continued economic decline and social destabilisation in the South. Against this background, cooperation between donor and recipient actors is faced with a duel uphill struggle. First, fewer resources can be mobilised to meet growing developmental needs. On the other hand, to organise and manage development policies and programmes in a result-oriented manner, grows more difficult. The threat of further aid cuts and of further drops of public support for providing aid become ever more real. A closer look at the organisational complexities and political constraints under which development cooperation is expected to perform effectively may help to improve current aid management approaches.

Towards Conceptual Clarity

At first sight, catchy definitions of what constitutes effective aid might appear attractive to use, in particular with regard to economic indicators. The term "aid effectiveness" is easily used in the same vein as "efficiency", "significance" or "impact" of aid. At times, obsession to measure and demonstrate the results of aid supported development processes can be observed among policy-makers and administrators on the donor side. Still the understanding of aid and its effectiveness as being part and parcel of a cooperation relationship between donor and recipient side parties, is scarcely embedded in practice. To determine how to make aid more effective requires more than a quick impact analysis of an individual and perhaps even isolated development project. Consequently, defining the concept of aid effectiveness needs to take into account at what levels cooperation is focused on. To strive for sustainable and effective modes of development cooperation will entail the need to combine recipient ownership of the development process with donor accountability concerns.

Performance expectations cannot be exclusively placed on the recipient while donor interests, their aid management systems and procedures remain unchanged.

An extended and more analytical, process-oriented definition should take into account four main aspects of aid effectiveness:

(a) Effective aid must relate to the building and/or strengthening of in-country aid management capacity;

(b) To maximise the degree of aid effectiveness, local ownership of the aid process is essential: from setting of priorities through policy formulation and

implementation onto the evaluation stages of the process;

(c) Increasing recipient side capabilities to take charge of aid relationship, will need to be combined with arrangements to meet legitimate donor accountability concerns;

(d) Aid effectiveness is a two-faceted objective: its realisation is equally dependent on increased transparency of donor motives and on dropping of non-developmental, political and economic aid objectiveness of donors.

In addition a broader range of stakeholders in the aid relationship needs to be actively involved: extending beyond accountable government and implementing agencies, to include democratic institutions and organisations of civil society and of the private sector.

Applying any definition of aid effectiveness without disaggregating macro-economic data and taking into account country specificity will only lead to unhelpful generalisations about aid and its effectiveness. It would seem more appropriate to adopt working definitions against which to assess effectiveness of aid resources at a country-specific level. On such a basis one could expect to arrive at more reliable indicators of how well aid resources contribute to improving developmental standards and meeting existing needs.

From Definition to Success—Key Requirements

Having reached agreement between the recipient and donor on what should constitute effectiveness of aid is only a starting point. Embarking on democratic, peaceful and participatory patterns of economic and social developments must follow: to arrive at significant and lasting improvement in many of the least developed countries will be a long-term process. This being said, it is crucial to design and implement such forms of development cooperation which involve a wide range of recipient side actors, not only from the government side but also from civil society at large. Seen as a process of increasing inclusion of intended beneficiaries of aid, the commitment to decentralise as well as entrust aid and its management grows in importance.

To fully capture Third World development realities, policy frameworks inspired by neoliberalist-type of development concepts and theories are grossly inadequate. The views and positions on aid articulated in the World Bank and the IMF, or in many if not most bilateral aid administrations in OECD countries, represent only one side of today's international cooperation, namely the donor side. The major weakness to point out with respect to this locus of debate, is a profound under representation if not even a total absence of recipient experiences and perceptions on aid in general and on its effectiveness in particular. There should be little doubt that ignoring to not actively identifying and involving such perceptions, leads to strongly donor driven aid.

To circumvent recipient side insights and views on strengths and weaknesses of aid strategies and mechanisms, will result in limited local commitment and sense of ownership over the aid process. Mutual decision-making between donors and recipients remains a rare policy approach. Aid procedures that are based on local management and less control-oriented donor roles in the aid process are still exceptions in development cooperation.

Structurally, in terms of the policy environment within which development aid is expected to function, the overriding policy framework is general based on structural adjustment policies (SAP). But the underlying conclusion made by proponents of SAPs that these policies induce aid effectiveness, has yet to be proven valid. It must suffice at this point to emphasize that there is no *a priori* relationship between world market integration under structural adjustment and sustainable development in poor countries.

Aid to these countries which is solely intended to reinforce fundamentally uneven and unequal patterns of world market integration should be scrutinised critically.

Some central issues need to be addressed in the course of improving aid and its effectiveness:

- institutional dimensions of aid relationships require strong policy-attention, both on the donor and the recipient side;
- capacities to effectively identify and formulate aid priorities need to be strengthened in recipient countries;
- local capacities to sustain reform efforts must be reinforced.

Levels of Intervention

If the design of aid and the terms upon which it is provided to a developing country are largely determined by the donor, the aid relationship can be characterised as essentially hierarchical. Recipient side views will rarely surface, as they are either not identified, or not well formulated. Possibilities of a recipient-led development strategies can be limited. Unless scope is provided to the recipient side actors to assume responsibilities, aid effectiveness is likely to remain low or fluctuating, and the sustainability of donor aid efforts will remain doubtful.

National planning processes and courses of national development in recipient countries should be seen as most effective where they are led under local responsibility and control. To arrive at this ideal situation, gaps need to be reduced and closed at the various intervention levels.

Donor aid resources provide valuable support for this process. Their effectiveness in meeting long-term objective of aid will need to be assessed on the basis of how well they perform at the different levels. Individual donors will expectedly perform differently at the various levels. What will prove to be the ultimate test for effectiveness is how well the donor aid performance accomplishes the broader objectives of development cooperation and how well it includes sustainable results.

In the analytical frameworks outlined here, development cooperation would seem to be confronted with the effectiveness gaps at the:

- *Structural Level:* International trade and investment patterns, debt problems and world market integration process appear as long-term constraining factors upon aid and its effectiveness;
- *Policy Level:* Dialogue and partnership in development cooperation are instrumental factors in recluding planning and co-ordination gaps with regard to policy analysis and formulation;
- *The Institutional Level* is where pertinent capacity gaps exist: capacity development efforts of donors and technical assistance measures play an important role in addressing weaknesses in aid effectiveness within a country's institutional setting;
- Finally, at the *level of aid projects (programmes),* it is generally the lack of sustainability of aid interventions which causes development activities to falter once donor support decreases or stops. In addition to technical cooperation, financial and material inputs serve to maintain project momentum and goal realisation. The issue of how to develop local capacity sufficiently in order for indigenous organisations to continue project activities initially supported by donor aid, remains the most important issue to address at this level.

Fostering Aid Effectiveness

In recent years donor aid budgets have been reshuffled, while having decreased in real terms. Geographical redistributions of reduced aid budgets have been accompanied by the need to accommodate rising emergency needs.

Additional resources to meet these needs have not been forthcoming: in general, aid budgets destined for developmental purposes have been under severe pressures while urgent humanitarian needs have added to the drain on resources.

Donor and recipient development efforts are too often isolated from one another, or poorly coordinated. They fail to address managerial and implementation bottlenecks. Cross-sectorial linkages, as well as interdisciplinary approaches to aid problems are only slowly gaining ground. It is increasingly obvious, that decisions on aid issues are subjected to concerns outside of the responsible ministry: finance ministers, economics ministers and unfortunately even defence ministers have a strong say in how much aid is to be provided, where it is to be concentrated and under what terms to be utilised. Inside of recipient countries, large portions of national budgets are allocated to non-development priorities with little or no impact on alleviating urgent poverty problems.

Development cooperation may make the biggest impact and be executed most effectively where donors and recipients agree upon multi-level aid strategies. To give an example, building a road to a remote rural area may well be done in an effective project manner. It is equally important to have a functioning transport authority in place to ensure maintenance of the roads. If this authority operates within a nationally defined infrastructure policy, best in accord with national trade and investment priorities, then the effectiveness of the project-level road building programme has a good chance of being high.

Institutional changes to set the stage for a profound reform process in development cooperation are needed. Reprioritising national budgets to reflect identified in country development needs may be one step. Setting up policy evaluation and formulation units can be complimentary measures. Deregulating markets and investment rules may serve to please donors, but dumping of cheap products which strangle local production efforts may easily result. Regional cooperation, including intensified South-South cooperation can provide some counterbalance. There are only a few areas where changes in the current system of development cooperation can occur, with a view to better manage the complexities of aid and the social, cultural, economic and political backgrounds against which they take place. The will and commitment to take policy action in both donor and recipient countries, through the broadest range of stakeholders and institutions as possible, will be the test for genuine efforts at improving development relations between North and South and organising cooperation effectively.

27

Economics and Environment

Statistics change our view of the world. So statistics, however objective and accurate, are never value free but focus on what societies deem important. For better or worse, they guide government, business and individual decisions.

Until recently, the old game of India's economic growth was unquestioned and the score was kept between the national players by comparing their Gross National Product (GNP) or its narrower domestic version, Gross Domestic Product (GDP). It is time to take a closer look at the proliferation of new scoreboards, statistics and quality-of-life indexes which will redefine wealth and progress and change the future direction of human society.

Clarifying Values

These new scorecards and the 'greening' of GNP/GDP national accounts reflect the new 'green' accounting in thousands of balance sheets, reports and books on environment. At the very least, assumptions underlying old and new indicators are being clarified. The debate is still over what rather than how to measure, and what to do about values and amenities that are priceless.

The costs of GNP growth arc now obvious—from felled forests, pollution exhausted soils, depleted natural resources and holes in the ozone layer to disrupted cultures and communities.

The concept of GNP/GDP was adapted into national accounting in India. With little re-examination, it continues to value bombs and bullets (defence expenditure), highly while setting the values of defence expenditure, education and public infrastructure—not to mention clean air and water and other environmental assets—at zero. It also ignores the some 50 per cent of production, which is unpaid—such as do-it-yourself home construction and repairs, food growing, household maintenance, parenting children and volunteering. In India such unpaid work can comprise upto 75 per cent of all production, particularly in agriculture sector.

Systems of National Accounts are based on GNP/GDP. Few economists, trade negotiators or development agencies questioned the basic assumption underlying it: that economies were generally in equilibrium, and that adding up a society's production and exchange of goods and services, measured in money terms, defined wealth and progress—however many social and environmental 'bads' came along with the 'goods'. Today's debates concern how best to calculate the costs of these 'bads' of production passed on to taxpayers or future generations. Some are easy to quantify: Costs of cleaning up pollution can be calculated, and their increase marches in lock-step with the expansion of pollution control and environment industry sectors.

Confusing means with ends: Indian Government officials, business executives, academics and hundreds of thousands of civic organisations are beginning to agree that we have been confusing means (i.e. GNP growth) with ends (human development and the survival and further evolution of our species under drastically changed planetary conditions).

New environmental and resource realities, legislation and insurance liabilities are driving further overhauling of traditional accounts. There is a big issue over whether new indicators will be weighted in money terms to expand GDP, or whether the separate components—health, education, environment, etc. - should be 'unbundled' so that the public can follow their own concern and hold politicians accountable for results:

Macro-economists still try to expand GDP by pricing environmental amenities and costs. Social and natural scientists, while agreeing that environmental amenities must be valued at more than zero in GDP, advocate 'unbundled' physical indicators, such as water and air quality measures and rates of infant mortality. They suspect that economists 'contingent prices' for valuing the environment are theoretical and arbitrary.

Such 'Shadow prices' are derived by ecomomists from historic welfare theories and formulas based on 'willingness to pay' (WTP) of willingness to be compensated'. Thus, to arrive at a price for valuing a marshland (one of the most productive ecosystems on the planet), economists could poll voters and residents with no motives other than appreciation for marshes and their non-monetary or aesthetic values or their desire to preserve them and the rare species they might contain. Such contingent prices would be lower than those offered by a hotel developer with profit motives or by a biotechnology firm which had identified species in the area that could be used for pharmaceutical products. Worse, such pricing discounts poor people's needs and concerns, since they cannot afford to participate. Here the price system should be subordinated to more democratic decision-making, such as voting on whether or not to protect the marsh.

Economic Accountability

Most social and natural scientists, as well as voters, believe that economics must now take its place within interdisciplinary teams of statisticians from health, education, energy and environmental policy fields. Economics is not a science by rigorous standards, but a profession often lacking in the quality assurances and accountability that governs lawyers and doctors. GNP is a malfunctioning strand of our 'cultural DNA code' - carrying erroneous information and signalling to the body-politic a form of growth analogous to that of cancer cells which consume the host's body. The new national accounting methods being redesigned to correct or even replace GNP/GDP will function like healthy' cultural

DNA strands', newly spliced in to govern healthier growth and more normal development patterns for human societies. Quantitative growth is dominant as children grow to adulthood, but once their mature size and weight are reached, this gives way to qualitative growth: education, social skills, broader awareness and even greater ethical understanding and wisdom. The statistical shift from GNP/GDP to sustainable development indicators mirrors such maturing of societies, recognising new goals and the traits human beings must now rapidly develop if we are to restructure our society for sustainability.

The new scorecards allow Indians to move beyond economism and ideologies of left and right to measure results directly and hold our business and government leaders accountable for implementing progress on the major goals of individual voters, consumers and investors. The new scorecards can help broaden trade pacts to include sustainable development criteria.

28

Population Growth and Energy

It has been scarcely 200 years—the dawn of the Industrial Revolution—since humans abandoned sole reliance on firewood, other biomass fuels, and direct sunlight to meet daily energy needs. In the past half-century, global demand for energy grew twice as fast as population, as industrial nations burned coal, oil and natural gas to fuel their economies. Over the next half-century, world's energy demands are projected to continue expanding beyond population growth, as developing countries try to catch up with industrial nations.

Developing countries will see tremendous growth in energy consumption in the next half-century, as growing populations and increasing affluence combine to drive their energy demands to dizzying levels. Based on projections from the U.S. Department of Energy and the Inter-governmental Panel on Climate Change, total energy consumption in the developing world will grow by 336 per cent—nearly three times faster than population—over the next 50 years, from 3,499 million tons of oil equivalent to 15,255 million tons. By 2030, energy consumption in the developing world will likely surpass usage in industrial nations.

Rising per capita consumption accounts for nearly two-thirds of the growth in energy demand in poorer nations, but different population trajectories can have dramatic effects on future demands. For example, assuming the same growth in per capita energy demand, moving to the low U.N.

population projection will reduce total energy demands from developing countries by 2,792 million tons of oil equivalent the output of nearly 3,000 average-sized coal-fired power plants.

In the next 50 years, the greatest growth in energy demands will come where economic activity is projected to be highest: In Asia, where consumption is expected to grow 361 per cent, though population will grow by just 50 per cent. Energy consumption in Latin America and Africa is projected to increase by 340 per cent and 326 per cent, respectively. Lower rates of population growth in Asia, compared with Latin America and Africa, mean that energy-use per person will increase most in Asia. Nonetheless, in all three regions, local pressures on energy sources, ranging from forests to fossil fuel reserves to waterways, will be significant.

When per capita energy consumption is high, even a low rate of population growth can have significant effect on total energy demand. In the United States, for example, where current per capita energy demand is nearly double that in other industrial nations and over 13 times that in developing countries, the 75 million people projected to be added in the next 50 years will boost energy demands by 758 million tons of oil equivalent, roughly the same as the present energy consumption of Africa and Latin America.

World energy-use per person doubled between 1950 and 1973, before confronting a short-term slowdown when restricted exports from oil-producing nations drove up energy prices. Another price shock, combined with a global economic recession, resulted in the slowdown of the early 1980s. The most recent stumbling block in energy growth followed the 1989 revolution in Eastern Europe, when energy-use in the former Soviet states plummeted. Although DOE and IPCC project substantial future growth, similar forces may act to check such a development.

World oil production per person reached a high in 1979 and has since declined 23 per cent. Moreover, estimates of when global oil production will peak range from 2011 by petroconsultants to 2025 by the IPCC, signalling future price shock as long as oil remains the world's dominant fuel. Although people born in 1950 saw per capita oil production quickly double in a few short decades, those born in 2000 are likely to see it cut in half, dropping below 1950 levels.

In addition, meeting increased energy demands will require more storage and transportation infrastructure. Communities without a reliable supply of clean water or an adequate system for waste disposal may also fall short in connection to power supplies. For the estimated 2 billion who are still off the grid, and also experiencing high rates of population growth, decentralised energy technologies, such as solar roof shingles and fuel cell power generators, are likely the most feasible and affordable option for meeting increased energy demands.

Yet it will not necessarily be the scarcity of fuel that constrains future growth in energy consumption, but rather concerns about climate change, air quality and water quality. Growing climate concerns will require massive reductions in fossil fuel use at a time when demand for energy is soaring. A shift to renewable energy sources, such as solar energy and wind power, in addition to continued efficiency gains for power plants, cars and appliances, holds great promise for meeting future energy demands without adverse ecological consequences.

❋❋❋

29

Population Growth and Urbanisation

The world's cities are growing far faster than its population. Indeed, aside from the growth of population itself, urbanisation is the dominant demographic trend of the half-century now ending. In 1950, 750 million of the world's people lived in cities. By 1996, this had at least tripled, to more than 2.6 billion. The number projected to live in cities by 2050, some 6.5 billion people, exceeds world population today.

Urbanisation on anything like the scale that we know today is historically quite recent. In 1800, only one city, London, had a million people. Today, 326 cities have at least that many people. And there are 14 mega cities, those with 10 million or more residents. Tokyo is the largest, at 27 million. Mexico city is second, at 17 million. New York city and Sao Paulo are close behind, with 16 million each. Rounding out the list in descending size are Bombay (15 million), Shanghai (14), Los Angeles (12), Calcutta (12), Buenos Aires (12), Beijing (11), Osaka (11), Lagos (10), Rio de Janeiro (10), and Delhi (10).

The rate of growth of cities in industrial countries during the first century or so of the Industrial Revolution was relatively slow. Today's cities are growing much faster. It took London 130 years to get from 1 million to 8 million. Mexico city made this jump in just 30 years.

Measured in annual growth, some cities, such as Lagos, Nigeria, are growing at 5 per cent a year; Bombay is growing at nearly 4 per cent. The world's urban population as a whole is growing by just over 1 million people each week. This urban growth is fed by natural increase of urban populations, by net migration from the countryside, and by villages, by net migration from the countryside, and by villages or towns expanding to the point where they become cities or they are absorbed by the spread of existing cities.

During the early stages of industrialisation, urbanisation was largely in response to the pull of employment opportunities in cities. More recently, however, the movement from countryside to city has been more the result of rural push than of urban pull. It is a reflection of the lack of opportunity in the countryside as already small plots of land are divided and then divided again with each passing generation, until they become so small that people can no longer make a living from them.

Historically, cities and the surrounding countryside had a symbolic relationship, with the latter supplying food and raw materials in exchange for manufactured products. Today, cities are tied much more to each other and to the global economy. The food and fuel that once came from the surrounding countryside now often comes from distant corners of the planet.

As societies urbanize, the use of basic resources, such an energy and water rises. In traditional rural societies, for example, people live on the land and thus do not need to travel to work. But once they migrate to cities, commuting becomes the rule, not the exception. In villages, most of the food that is consumed is produced locally, requiring little energy for processing, packaging, and transportation; once people move into cities, on the other hand, virtually all their food must be brought in. In a village where residents typically draw their water from a central well and carry it to their homes, water use in necessarily limited. But when villagers move to urban high-rise apartment buildings with indoor plumbing, replete with showers and flush toilets, water consumption soars.

The ecology of cities is a continuing challenge to city managers simply because cities require the concentration of huge quantities of water, food, energy and raw materials. The waste products must then be dispersed or the city will become uninhabitable. As cities become larger, the disposal of residential and industrial wastes becomes ever more challenging.

Partly as a result of the mounting pressure for people to migrate to cities, the growth in urban populations is far out stripping the availability of basic services, such as water, sewerage, transportation, and electricity. As a result, life in urban shantytowns is plagued by poverty, pollution, congestion, homelessness, and unemployment.

Since the beginning of the Industrial Revolution, the terms of trade between countryside and city have favoured the latter simply because cities control the scarce resources in development, namely capital and technology. But if the price of food rises in the years ahead, as now seems likely, the terms of trade could shift, favouring the countryside. If in the new world of the twenty-first century the scarce resources are land and water, those controlling them could have the upper hand in determining rural/urban terms of trade.

This aside, if recent trends continue, within the next several years more than half of us will be living in cities—making the world more urban than rural for the first time in history. We will have become an urban species, far removed from our hunter-gatherer origins.

***

30

Finance Matters

Financial Liberalisation Too Much Too Soon?

An efficient and stable financial system is important for economic growth and poverty reduction. The financial crises that have afflicted many countries in recent times have been a costly and painful reminder of the disastrous consequences for development of weak financial markets. The recurrence of financial crises, at both the international and national levels, and the adverse effect they have had on economic growth and poverty levels, have highlighted the need for a policy framework which addresses the inherent vulnerability of financial markets to systemic instability and failure.

Governments have always intervened in the financial sector and there are sound theoretical and practical reasons for doing so. Financial markets are characterised by problems of limited and unequal information, making them inherently imperfect and prone to failure. Financial regulation and supervision are therefore essential for efficient and stable financial market development. How should governments intervene? Have financial liberalisation and financial sector reform made financial systems more, or less vulnerable to instability and systemic crises? How can the process be better managed? What is the best policy framework for supporting financial sector development in low-income countries.

Repression to Liberalisation

For many years, governments followed a policy of financial 'repression', which relied on fixing interest rates below market levels and controlling the allocation of credit. The economic distortions induced by these policies were considerable. Financial systems remained under developed, lending patterns were inefficient and failed to achieve their distributional goals. Negative real interest rates led to low savings and encouraged capital flight. Macro economic performance also deteriorated countries with large negative real interest rates experienced lower location efficiency and growth rates. In the state owned banking sector, poor lending decisions (often politically influenced) and low repayment rates led to bank insolvency and large budgetary bailouts of depositors and creditors.

A growing awareness of the economic costs of financial 'repression', led to financial 'liberalisation' as the dominant policy paradigm over the past two decades. Initially, the relaxation of controls on interest rates was the focus for financial reform which was often triggered by a financial crisis. The relaxation of controls on the financial sector was often part of a more general policy shift towards liberalisation of the domestic economy and opening out the international economy liberalisation soon broadened therefore beyond interest rate liberalisation, to include a wide range of measures constituting a programme of financial sector reform was adopted under World Bank sectoral or structural adjustment lending conditionalities, the key elements of which included privatisation of banks, entry of new domestic and foreign entrants in to the banking sector, bank restructuring and recapitalisation, opening upto the capital account, strengthening bank regulation and supervision institutions.

Has Financial Liberalisation Worked

The period of financial liberalisation conincided with, or was soon followed by heightened financial instability, culminating in the dramatic financial crisis in East Asia in the second-half of the 1990s. Clearly, financial liberalisation has not led to a smooth transition to a stable and efficient financial system. It would be wrong, however, to jump to the easy, but shallow, conclusion that financial liberalisation has 'failed'. Firstly, the fact that the period of increased systemic instability does not prove causality. Secondly, no process of change comes cheap: a reasoned assessment of the costs and benefits of the policy changes is needed. And thirdly, what would have been the outcome without the policy change. Finally the impact of financial liberalisation will differ between countries, depending on each country's economic and institutional characteristics. The more relevant research issue, therefore, relates to the design and timing of context-specific policy measures, which will contribute to the development of an efficient and stable financial system. Could financial liberalisation have been managed better? If so, what policies are now needed? The commercial banks are the dominant component of the financial sector in low-income countries and are critical to the efficiency and stability of the financial system as a whole. Financial liberalisation was associated with a shift in prudential regulation from direct regulation of banks, by for example, regular site visits, to an indirect approach based on the monitoring of bank capital to ensure that it remained adequate in relation to the risk being taken. Additional regulatory measures are also necessary to restrain the activities of the privitised and other newly-established private banks. The regulatory and supervisory framework may also need to be extended, to cover micro-finance institutions which have developed significant deposit taking capacity.

Four main obstacles to efficient banking regulations are:

(a) information, contracting and monitoring problems;

(b) Lack of supervisory personnel;

(c) High operational costs; and

(d) Poor credibility and regulation of regulatory bodies. The appropriateness of various policy measures for dealing with these constraints are discussed and ranked in terms of their suitability for low-income countries. What are the implications of allowing micro-finance institutions to offer a range of financing services beyond small-scale lending.

Too Much, Too Soon?

The experience with financial liberalisation reveals a strong correlation between liberalisation and financial crisis. This can be explained partly by the exposure of existing inefficiencies and distortions in the financial structure, and partly by a failure to develop a strong regulatory and supervisory framework, prior to liberalisation. Weakness in the initial conditions affect the ability of the privatised banks and new market entrants, to operate on broadly commercial principles. Borrowers are often unable to service their loans, due to poor quality lending and high interest rates. Liberalisation of the capital account increases the inflow of foreign capital, but at the same time threatens that stability of the financial institutions by increasing the exchange rate and domestic lending risks.

The existing regulatory and supervisory system may be unsuited to a market-based environment. Consequently, across-the-broad 'big-bang' financial liberalisation and financial sector reform increase the likelihood of systemic crisis, where the institutional and human resource environment is weak. Much of the blame for post-liberalisation financial crisis lies, therefore, with the scale and sequencing of financial reform. What is needed is a more gradual and considered approach to financial liberalisation, which recognises that institutional strengthening, especially in the regulation and supervision capacity, is a prerequisite and supervision capacity is a prerequisite for creating a more efficient and stable financial sector which can contribute fully to achieving economic growth and poverty reduction in developing countries.

❋❋❋

31

The Biggest Industry the World has Ever Seen

The Future of World Tourism

The year 2020 will see the penetration of technology into all aspects of life. It will become possible to live one's days without exposure to other people, according to WTO's latest look into the future.

But this bleak prognosis has a silver lining for the tourism sector. People in the high-tech future will crave the human touch and tourism will be the principal means to achieve this.

Tourism companies that manage to provide "high-touch" products will prosper. Upscale, luxury services that pamper and spoil their customers have a bright future in the upcoming century. But WTO's report also predicts good prospects for low-budget destinations and packages. Self-catering holiday facilities, for example, which offer plenty of opportunities for socializing among families and friends. Opportunities abound at both ends of the spectrum and there will be plenty of them.

$5 Billion a Day Industry

WTO's study Tourism: 2020 Vision predicts 1.5 billion tourists will be visiting foreign countries annually by the year 2020, spending more that US $2 trillion - or US $5 billion every day. These forecasts represent nearly three times more international tourists than the 66 m million recorded in 1999 and nearly five times more tourism spending, which last year topped US $453 billion. Tourist arrivals are predicted to grow by an average 4.3 per cent a year over the next two decades, while receipts from international tourism will climb by 6.7 per cent a year.

To factor in domestic tourism, WTO multiplies arrivals by 10 and quadruples receipts, which brings us to the grant totals of 16 billion tourists spending US $8 trillion in 2020.

Tourism in the 21st century will not only be the world's biggest industry, it will be the largest by far that the world has ever seen. Along with its phenomenal growth and size, the tourism industry will also have to take on more responsibility for its extensive impacts. Not only its economic impact, but also its impact on the environment, on societies and on cultural sites, all of which will be increasingly scrutinized by governments, consumer groups and the travelling public.

We hope that Tourism 2020 Vision will be more than a useful marketing tool, that it will act as a warning signal for destinations—helping them recognize the need to prepare for the pressure of growth, WTO is advising destinations to implement long-term, strategic planning and to strengthen the partnerships, both strategically and at the operational level, between the public and private sectors.

Growth of Long-Haul

Tourism: 2020 Vision indicates that tourists of the 21st century will be travelling further a field on their holidays, often to China and even to outer space. The percentage of long-haul travel is predicted to increase from 18 per cent in 1995 to 24 per cent by 2020.

Tourism companies looking to cash in on this booming sector are advised to look towards Asia. China will be the world's number one destination by the year 2020 and it will also become the fourth most important generating market. Currently it does not even figure among the world's destinations predicted to make great strides in the tourism industry are Russia, Hong Kong, Thailand, Singapore, Indonesia and South Africa.

Short pleasure voyages to outer space will become a reality by 2004 or 2005, according to the study carried out by WTO Statistics Chief Enzo Pad in consultation with 85 governments and 50 tourism visionaries.

It is expected space trips will last up to four days and cost on average US $100,000. NASA, the US space agency, has recently surveyed the travel industry for interest in space tourism and some US companies are already taking reservations and deposits from private citizens hoping to become the first tourists in outer space.

But while some travellers may be suiting up for space voyages, the vast majority of the world's population will never leave their own countries, not even by the year 2020.

Only 7 per cent of the world's population will be travelling internationally by the year 2020, up from 3.5 per cent in 1996—but still just the tip of the ice berg.

European Trends

"Tourism: 2020 Vision" predicts that Europe will remain by far the leading inbound tourism region as well as the main generator of international tourists. International arrivals in Europe will reach 717 million by 2020? more than twice as many as last year.

Overall, tourism to Europe is predicted to grow more slowly than the world average; at a rate of 3.1 per cent annually, though some countries will fare better than others. Central and Eastern European countries will become the new motor for Europe, feeding and being fed by other European and long-haul generating markets. Tourism to Central and Eastern Europe will grow by 4.8 per cent a year and the former Soviet Block countries will surpass 200 million arrivals by 2016—a doubling in last 15 years.

The Eastern Mediterranean countries of Cyprus, Turkey and Israel are also expected to show good growth of 4.6 per cent a year. Tourism to the United Kingdom is forecast to grow by 4 per cent annually, just under the world average. Reflecting world patterns and increasing air travel, Europeans will be taking trips more frequently and further from home. Total outbound travel from European countries is predicted to reach 771 million trips a year by 2010, again more than twice as many as last year.

Long-haul travel to countries outside of Europe will grow by 6.1 per cent a year in the upcoming decades to reach 15 per cent of all trips taken by Europeans or 115,600,000 departures. Long-haul currently accounts for 12 per cent of European outbound travel or about 42 million trips a year.

Since the typical European tourist who spends his holiday at the beach will be more frequently choosing Asian or Caribean resorts, European beach destinations are advised to orientate their product development and marketing increasingly to new tourist sources, especially Japan, the newly industrialized countries of Asia and the Americas.

Mature European destinations will have continually to strive to seek product and market differentiation to avoid a tired 'or stale image in major generating markets.

Recipe for Success

While growth of the tourism industry will be unstoppable In the 21st century, increased benefits cannot be taken for granted. Competition among destinations will also become increasingly fierce.

The study Tourism: 2020 Vision outlines a series of 12 mega trends that will shape the sector and offers advice on how to better compete. No destination or tourism operator can afford to sit back and wait for more tourists to arrive. They have to be won—and there will be winners and losers. To be a winner, there are a number of imperatives

1. Development focused on quality and sustainability.
2. Value-for-money.

3. Full utilization of information technology to identify and communicate effectively with market segments and niches.

Product development and marketing will need to match each other more closely, based on the main travel motivators of the 21st century. Tourism: 2020 Vision calls these motivating factors the Three E's - Entertainment, Excitement and Education.

The study also highlights the importance of image in a tourists' selection of a holiday destination in the future. While an image of safety and security is already an important deciding factor for tourists, holiday makers of the 21st century will be looking for places with a trendy image.

As 2020 Vision points out, the next century will mark the emergence the tourism destinations as 'a fashion accessory'. The choice of holiday destination will help define the identity of the travellers and, in an increasingly homogeneous world, set him apart from the hordes of other tourists.

Boutique destinations and space agencies beware! You are on the threshold of meeting the 21st century tourist.

***

32

The Dematerialisation of the World Economy

The first Industrial Revolution marked the transition from robber-and-plunder colonialism to the systematic development of the "overseas" territories in the framework of an international division of labour between raw material suppliers and manufacturers of finished goods. There was an "historic integration" of the colonised areas in the development of their parent-states. What will the third Industrial Revolution do for the Third World ? Will it now come to an "historic separation"?

The end of the East-West conflict was reason enough to talk about a radical change in world politics. But at the same time an upheaval in the world economy is taking place that possibly will have even wider impacts. As a reference point for the following thoughts, three dimensions of this change are pointed out:

1. the upgrading of processing information rather than materials as object of economic activity (technological dimension);

2. the evolvement of global communications networks (socio-cultural dimension);

3. the change of the nature of work (socio-economic dimension).

All three dimensions can be summarised under the buzzphrase "tertialisation of the world economy."

In that respect, talk of the "Third Industrial Revolution" is misleading. It is not about a third epoch of industrialisation, but about the beginning of a de-industrialisation, the transition from the industrial to the information society.

Historic Separation?

In the 1960s and early 1970s, there was often talk of the Third World as the Third Sector of the world economy. Also then the Third World was not much more than an "imaginary community". But as such it had a certain significance in world politics. This implied not only its strategic role in the East-West conflict and its ideological function as the supporter of different "third paths" between capitalism and socialism. It was also about the Third World's attested "chaos power". That linked the fear (in the North) and the hope (in the South) that the developing countries would be in a position to cut-off the industrial nations from supplies of important raw materials, thus putting them under pressure. But it was soon seen that both sides had over estimated this possibility, even with regard to oil. Instead of supply bottlenecks arising, raw materials prices plummeted. For some commodities, the fall in prices exceeded those of the Great Depression of 1929/30.

This was due, *inter alia,* to the conjunction of lower demand from the industrial nations and expansion of production by the raw materials suppliers. Business activities dependent upon the supply of raw materials are tending to lose importance compared with the overall development of the global economy. The reason for this is to be seen in the transition from a material to an information economy.

This transition is taking place in line with the revolutionising of data transmission and the expansion of financial transactions which are not directly related to changes in the production of materials. The speed of the changes is remarkable.

However, the dematerialisation of business activities does not lead to decoupling of the Third World from the world economy. Declining market shares in world trade are not the expression of separation, but a loss of the affected countries positions in the world economy. Thus, the impact of dematerialisation is "only" that the negotiating positions of raw materials suppliers vis-a-vis the industrial nations will deteriorate further.

Differentiation of the Third World

But the radical change in the global economy is affecting some developing countries worse than others. Sub-saharan Africa and some countries in West and South Asia and Latin America are being pushed back further. The oil-producing countries with their high per capita export earnings will be able to hold their positions in the world economy for some time to come. The threshold countries of East and South-East Asia can expand theirs so long as they can continue to attract a growing share of global industrial production, and at the same time participate in the tertialisation of the world economy in the shape of rapidly-growing financial transactions. Thereby it should be noted that the degree of tertialisation in itself is not an adequate indicator for economic avant-gardism. Brazil exhibits a high degree of tertialisation in combination with a low macro-economic development dynamics. A good part of its tertialisation is being achieved by speculative financial transactions with their inherently greater risks and uncertainties than in the industrial countries. Such dangers have been demonstrated by Mexico's peso crisis and its repercussions on the whole of Latin America.

In some Third World countries, a "location annuity" has replaced the old raw materials one. Here it's about providing locations for off-shore transactions which offer international capital traders a maximum of freedom of movement combined with low taxation. Suitable for such operations are small countries which, despite low levy rates, achieve significant income in macro-economic terms.

The radical changes in the world economy are spurring the differentiation of the Third World without, however, necessarily fostering a dissolution of the Third World as an "imaginary community". It is precisely the advanced countries of East and South-East Asia that are showing a certain interest in the formulation of joint positions of the "South" in order to secure their own positional gains in the global economy. It's not by chance that the non-aligned countries and the Group of 77 have formed a joint coordination committee, and that the ASEAN countries are changing course on the international human rights policy.

Hitherto, the developing countries' strategy was to broaden the concept of human rights as a justification for demands on the industrial nations. But of late some developing countries, led by the ASEAN states, have questioned the universal validity of human rights even after their universality was confirmed by consensus at the Conference on Human Rights in Vienna in 1993. Playing a role in this policy is the governments' fear that due to the expansion of global communications networks, the behaviour patterns and preferences of their own people could in some way become similar to those of the West. As the rulers see it, that would be detrimental to the continuation of the development models practised so far.

Internet Creates New Cultural Dimension

Much information which Asian governments view as subversive in already globally available on the Internet. The old. struggle over the world information order, which at first was primarily a clinch between East and West, is thus taking on a new dimension. For with the growing importance of computer literacy to a country's ability to assert itself on world markets, the Asian threshold countries have not only an interest in controlling the online communication but also to expand it and the know-how that it requires.

Even the critics of any interventions in the internet and other global communications networks must admit that modern communications technologies are politically blind and their use in itself does not represent progress. The setting up and expansion of global information highways will offer forum not only to people who want to use it for education and enlightenment, but also to all shades of fundamentalists. These highways will not necessarily bring the misery of many Third World regions closer to the industrial countries, but possibly rather strengthen the tendency to process all world events as entertainment.

Global Two-Thirds Society

The gravest aspect of the current upheaval in the world economy is its negative impact on jobs. The information economy needs for fewer workers than an economy based on materials. Instead, the demands on the skills of the workers are growing. Twenty per cent of the world workforce will in future be employed as (overworked) "intelligence workers". Eighty per cent will work part-time, if they are not underemployed or jobless. So the tertialisation of the global economy delivers more underemployment rather than more leisure time. The workers who are rationalised out of their jobs in the industrial sector cannot be absorbed by the service sector because it, too, is not left untouched by rationalisation measures. The civil service is also cutting back on staff. At all levels, there's a race to make the greatest possible savings on payrolls. At the same time, there's growing pressure to cut costs in providing for the victims of this development. That means thinning out the social security safety net.

The bottom line is that the two-thirds society, which developmental action groups hitherto assumed was limited to the Third World, is spreading worldwide. That, however, will not in the foreseeable future lead to an amendment of the North-South disparities. It's true that the change in the global economy is taking place faster, and to a greater extent in the industrial nations. But rationalisation is also happening in the developing countries in a bid to boost their competitiveness. So the upheaval in the world economy aggravates the problems which exist in a majority of the developing countries, while creating new ones in the industrial nations. The need for action on the North-South policy is growing, among the industrial nations. The need for action on the North-South Policy is growing, while the industrial nations' scope for concessions and compromises is shrinking. The new social question which is now crystallizing at global level is not being answered. The consequences are unforeseeable.

Another Loser?

It's more probable that a sharpening of the North-South confrontation is to be reckoned with. For the industrial nations will attempt to keep the social costs of the information economy at bay for as long as possible. The trade unions will thereby compete with the developing countries for jobs for their members. But this policy has its limits precisely because of the peaking of the problems in the industrial nations. Overstepping these limits means war and passively accepting them chaos and social decay. Solutions could be sought in two directions: effective taxation of the information economies and the creation of jobs in the non-profit sector. But it's possible there are no global solutions for global problems. That would mean for at least part of the Third World a renewal of the old debate on partial decoupling from the world economy.

❊ ❊ ❊

Bibliography

De Soto, H., 1990, *The Other Path: The Invisible Revolution in the Third World,* Reprint edition, New York: Harper Collins.

Doha Development Agenda, 2001, *The Ministerial Declaration and other Decisions and Declarations from the Doha Ministerial Conference,* Available: httpa/www.wto.org/english/tradop_e/dda_e/dda_e.htm.

English, P., B. Hoekman, and A. Mattoo, 2002, *Development, Trade and the WTO: A Handbook.* The World Bank, Washington D.C.

Feketekuty, G., 1988, *International Trade in Services: An Overview and Blueprint for Negotiations.* Cambridge, MA: American Enterprise Institute/Ballinger,

Finger, J.M., 1993, *Antidumping: How it Works and Who Gets Hurt,* Ann Arbor: Univ. of Michigan Press.

Finger, J.M., 2001, "Implementing the Uruguay Round Agreements: Problems for Developing Countries," *The World Economy* 24 (9 September), pp. 1097-108.

Finger, J.M. and J.J. Nogues, 2001, *The Unbalanced Uruguay Round Outcome: The New Areas in Future WTO Negotiations,* Policy Research Working Paper No. 2732, The World Bank, Washington, D.C.

Finger, J.M. and L. Schuknecht, 2001, "Market Access Advances and Retreats: The Uruguay Round and Beyond," In B. Hoekman and W. Martin, eds., *Developing Countries and the WTO: A Proactive Agenda,* Oxford: UK and Malden. Also available as Policy Research Working Paper No. 2232 at http://www.worldbank.org/researcl/ trade.

Finger, J.M. and P. Schuler, 2000, "Implementation of Uruguay Round Commitments: The Development Challenge," *The World Economy* 23(4, April), pp. 511-25. Also available as Policy Research Working Paper No. 2215 at http://www.worldbank.org/research/trade.

Finger, J.M. and L.A. Winters, 2002, "Reciprocity." In P. English, B. Hoekman, and A. Mattoo, *Development, Trade and the WTO: A Handbook,* The World Bank, Washington D.C. Finger, J.M., M.D. Ingco, and U. Reincke, 1996, *The Uruguay Round: Statistics on Tariff Concessions Given and Received,* The World Bank, Washington, D.C.

Finger, J.M., F. Ng, and S. Wangchuk, 2001, *Antidumping as Safeguard Policy,* Policy Research Working Paper No. 2730, The World Bank, *Washington,* D.C.

Francois, J.F., B. McDonald, and H. Nordstrom, 1996, "The Uruguay Round: A Numerically Based Qualitative Assessment." In *W.* Martin and L.A. Winters, eds., *The Uruguay Round and the Developing Countries,* Cambridge: Cambridge University Press.

Harrison, G.W., T.F. Rutherford, and D.G. Tarr, 1996, "Quantifying the Uruguay Round." In W. Martin and L. A. Winters, eds., *The Uruguay Round and the Developing Countries,* Cambridge: Cambridge University Press.

Hudec, R.E., 1970. "The GATT Legal System: A Diplomat's Jurisprudence," *Journal of World Trade Law 4,* pp. 615-65.

International Intellectual Property Alliance (IIPA), 2002a, *Description of the IIPA,* Available: http://www.iipa.com/ aboutiipa.html.

International Intellectual Property Alliance (IIPA), 2002b, *Statistics,* Available: http:www.iipa.com/statistics.html.

Martin, W. and L.A. Winters, 1996, *The Uruguay Round and the Developing Countries,* Cambridge: Cambridge University Press.

Martin, W. and L.A. Winters, 1996, "The Uruguay Round: A Milestone for the Developing Countries." In W. Martin and L.A. Winters, eds., *The Uruguay Round and the Developing Countries,* Cambridge: Cambridge University Press.

Maskus, K.E., 2000, *Intellectual Property Rights in the Global Economy,* Institute for International Economics, Washington, D.C.

Michalopoulos, C., 1999, "The Developing Countries in the WTO," *The World Economy* 22(1) January.

O'Neill, T. and G. Hymel (contributor), 1995, *All Politics is Local: And Other Rules of the Game,* Reprint edition. Massachusetts: Adams Media Corporation.

Panagariya, A., Forthcoming, "Developing Countries at Doha: A Political Economy Analysis", *The World Economy.*

Petersen, M. and D.G. McNeil Jr., 2001, "Maker Yielding Patent in Africa for AIDS Drug", *The New York Times,* 15 March, p. 1.

Preeg, E.H., 1995, *Traders in a Brave New World,* Chicago and London: University of Chicago Press.

Reichman, J.H., 1998, "Securing Compliance with the TRIPs Agreement after US v India." *Journal of International Economic Law* (1, December), pp. 603-06.

Ricupero, R., 2000, *A Development Round: Converting Rhetoric Into Substance.* Paper presented at the Symposium on Efficiency, Equity and Legitimacy: The Multilateral Trading System at the Millennium, 1-2 June, John F. Kennedy School of Government, Harvard University, Cambridge, Massachusetts.

Shaffer, G., 2002, *The Law-in Action of International Trade Litigation: The Blurring of the Public and the Private.* University of Wisconsin Law School, Madison. Manuscript.

Winham, G., 1986, *International Trade and The Tokyo Round of Negotiations,* Princeton: Princeton University Press.

Winters, L.A., 2002, *Doha and the World Poverty Targets,* Paper prepared for the Annual Bank Conference on Development Economics (ABCDE), 29-30 April, World Bank, Washington, D.C.

World Bank, 2002, *Global Economic Prospects and the Developing Countries,* The World Bank, Washington D.C.

World Trade Organization (WTO), 2002a, *WTO Secretariat Budget for 2002,* Available: http://www.wto.org/english/thewto_e/secre_e/budget_e.htm.

2002b, *Pledging Conference to Provide Sound Financial Basis for Doha Agenda,* available: http://www.wto.org/english/news_e/pres02_e/pr277_e.htm.

Zeller, T.W., 1992, *American Trade and Power in the 1960s,* New York: Columbia.

INDEX